ADVANCE PRAISE FOR

## *Effective Lecturing*

"I am pleased to strongly recommend 'Effective lecturing'. This book not only very successfully presents a case for lecturing, emphasising student engagement, but also highlights macro and micro level skills required to lecture well, providing clear principles and examples. The exercises provided are extremely valuable for those wishing to fully understand the value of the book."
—Ramon Lewis, Emeritus Professor, School of Education, La Trobe University, Bundoora, Victoria 3086, AUSTRALIA Author of the Developmental Management Approach to Classroom Behavior: Responding to individual Needs.

"Unlike most books on teaching, this book focuses on research-based teaching methods that are perfect for anyone learning how to teach or who wants to refine their teaching skills. 'Effective lecturing' is a perfect book that explains the research behind each strategy and the strategy itself in a way that makes it easier for anyone to understand."
—Kent Divoll, Associate Professor, College of Education, University of Houston-Clear Lake.

"The book 'Effective lecturing' explains the most important concepts, skills and abilities for knowledge transfer, which are often neglected by us university lecturers. The content of the book is scientific, professional, comprehensive and clearly structured and written. It is very easy to find your way around while reading and you will discover valuable information. I recommend the book for all teachers, trainers and those interested in the subject."
—Yuhan Huang, Assistant Professor, Guangdong University of Foreign Studies, Canton, China

# Effective Lecturing

Andreas Rupp

# Effective Lecturing

## Communicating and presenting subject content

PETER LANG

New York · Berlin · Bruxelles · Chennai · Lausanne · Oxford

Library of Congress Cataloging-in-Publication Data

Names: Rupp, Andreas, author.
Title: Effective lecturing : communicating and presenting subject content / Andreas Rupp.
Description: New York, NY : Peter Lang, [2025] | Includes index.
Identifiers: LCCN 2024031311 (print) | LCCN 2024031312 (ebook) | ISBN 9781636679327 (paperback) | ISBN 9781636679303 (pdf) | ISBN 9781636679310 (epub)
Subjects: LCSH: Lectures and lecturing.
Classification: LCC PN4193.L4 R87 2025 (print) | LCC PN4193.L4 (ebook) | DDC 808.5/1–dc23/eng/20240828
LC record available at https://lccn.loc.gov/2024031311
LC ebook record available at https://lccn.loc.gov/2024031312
DOI 10.3726/b22126

Bibliographic information published by the Deutsche Nationalbibliothek. The German National Library lists this publication in the German National Bibliography; detailed bibliographic data is available on the Internet at http://dnb.d-nb.de.

Cover design by Peter Lang Group AG

ISBN 9781636679327 (paperback)
ISBN 9781636679303 (ebook)
ISBN 9781636679310 (epub)
DOI 10.3726/b22126

© 2025 Peter Lang Group AG, Lausanne
Published by Peter Lang Publishing Inc., New York, USA
info@peterlang.com—www.peterlang.com

All rights reserved.
All parts of this publication are protected by copyright.
Any utilization outside the strict limits of the copyright law, without the permission of the publisher, is forbidden and liable to prosecution.
This applies in particular to reproductions, translations, microfilming, and storage and processing in electronic retrieval systems.

This publication has been peer reviewed.

# Foreword

In today's knowledge society, it is crucial to be able to present information clearly, concisely, and convincingly.

This book is a guide for anyone who wants to present their expertise and content effectively, efficiently, interestingly, and humorously. Whether at school, university, or in a company, effective lecturing and skills are key to success.

The following chapters present established and tested methods as well as new techniques that will help you structure your content and inspire your audience.

The content of the book is described using key components that are necessary to teach subject content effectively and appropriately. These include planning, structure, clarity, motivation, interest, engagement, and creating a positive atmosphere.

Specific behaviors for these key components are presented and described. Select some of these behaviors and use them consciously.

Many of the concepts and behaviors described here have been systematically researched over many years and implemented and evaluated in training programs. The results have been published in scientific publications and presented at international conferences.

My aim is to provide you with a practical guide to help you get your message across clearly and comprehensibly, inspire your audience, and highlight your expertise.

I hope that this book will provide you with valuable insights and suggestions for developing your lecturing and presentation skills and using them successfully.

# Notes on reading

The transfer of knowledge in the form of lectures, presentations, direct instruction, and instruction is an essential feature of education and training in all educational institutions worldwide.

However, to achieve effective and sustainable communication of basic knowledge as well as technical and scientific content, various factors are required, such as a clear structure of the content and the involvement of the audience.

In addition to the individual, the social nature of people is always at the forefront of knowledge transfer, as every form of communication in humans is dependent on cooperation—and this also applies to knowledge transfer through lectures or presentations. Without mutual tacit agreement with the audience, it is not possible to impart knowledge and content.

Using the various opportunities for social interaction with those present during a lecture also increases the acquisition and consolidation of knowledge and learning objects and, if the material is presented well, the mutual enjoyment of the topic.

Therefore, four aspects have influenced the selection and presentation of this book to describe how knowledge can be effectively and sustainably conveyed in the form of lectures and presentations:

1. The basics of communication are presented to provide a better understanding of why the transmission and exchange of knowledge is one of the outstanding, unique cultural and cognitive abilities of humans to enable cooperative action and expand knowledge, as well as the importance of a common background of knowledge and experience.
2. Effective skills and interactive approaches are presented that help the audience receive and process information. This includes the ability to present information in a clear and structured way, to arouse interest and attention for a topic, and to create an atmosphere in which people enjoy listening.
3. Another guiding principle of the book is the diversity of methods. To be effective and sustainably interactive, forms of lectures and instruction require a combination with other methods. For this reason, methods such as individual work, small-group work, the case method, and controlled discussion are presented to make lectures or presentations interactive and thus improve motivation and retention.
4. The evaluated training program "Interactive and adaptive teaching of subject content" is presented and described with the associated behavioral dimensions, as well as concrete, effective, and appropriate behaviors. The training program combines various methods, such as direct instruction, practice with questions and guided individual work, in consideration of the different abilities of learners and audiences, and improves the motivation and retention performance of learners through interactive elements.
5. This book is intended as a workbook and is primarily written for self-study. I have tried to keep the complex simple. This has resulted in some scientific vagueness here and there, which may be appreciated by all who read the book.
6. Most chapters begin with a table, on which you will find the essential terms used in the chapter and what they are needed for. There are exercises for many sections. They are identified by this symbol:

# Contents

List of figures     xv
List of tables     xvii

Part I Effective communication and presentation of subject content
1 Conceptual framework for the communication of knowledge and culture     3
    1.1 Language as a unique social and cognitive skill     3
    1.2 Teaching methods for imparting knowledge     4
    1.3 Arguments for and against imparting knowledge in the form of lectures and presentations     6
    1.4 Integration of various components for effective lecturing and knowledge transfer     7
2 Planning and contextual factors for the preparation of a lecture     9
    2.1 Learning objectives     9
       2.1.1 Specific learning objectives     10
       2.1.2 Steps for determining learning objectives     11
    2.2 Target audience     11
    2.3 External conditions     13

| | | |
|---|---|---|
| 3 | Behavioral dimensions in imparting knowledge | 15 |
| | 3.1 The effectiveness and appropriateness of communicative skills | 17 |
| 4 | Behavioral dimension: Clarity | 19 |
| | 4.1 Sub-dimension: Forms of organization | 19 |
| |     4.1.1 External structure of a lecture through formal outline features | 20 |
| |     4.1.2 Internal structure of a lecture through consistency | 21 |
| | 4.2 Sub-dimension: Basic structures | 22 |
| |     4.2.1 Hierarchical structure | 22 |
| |     4.2.2 Linear sequential structure | 24 |
| |     4.2.3 Network structure | 27 |
| | 4.3 The clarity of execution | 28 |
| |     4.3.1 Skills that promote the development of a clear structure at the beginning of a lecture | 29 |
| |     4.3.2 Skills that promote thinking and understanding of the content during a lecture | 31 |
| |     4.3.3 Skills that promote clarity in the execution | 36 |
| |     4.3.4 Skills for all phases of the lecture | 40 |
| 5 | Behavioral dimension: Motivation and interest | 47 |
| | 5.1 Sub-dimensions: Individual interest and situational interest | 47 |
| | 5.2 Skills for the individual interest sub-dimension | 48 |
| |     5.2.1 Refer to talents and individual interests | 48 |
| |     5.2.2 Referring to fears | 48 |
| |     5.2.3 Refer to the motivation to participate | 49 |
| |     5.2.4 Demonstrate the relevance of the lecture content | 49 |
| |     5.2.5 Promoting inner motivation | 49 |
| |     5.2.6 Interacting with individuals | 50 |
| |     5.2.7 Creating "aha" experiences | 50 |
| | 5.3 Skills for situational interest sub-dimension | 50 |
| |     5.3.1 Creating meaningful events through good preparation | 51 |
| |     5.3.2 Creating meaningful events through technical systems | 53 |
| |     5.3.3 Creating meaningful events through verbal vividness | 55 |
| |     5.3.4 Creating meaningful events through enthusiasm and non-verbal liveliness | 58 |
| 6 | Behavioral dimension: Social learning climate and social atmosphere | 61 |
| | 6.1 Sub-dimension: Control | 62 |
| |     6.1.1 Dominance | 63 |
| |     6.1.2 Social-integrative lecturing | 63 |
| |     6.1.3 Submission | 66 |

|       |       |                                                              |     |
|-------|-------|--------------------------------------------------------------|-----|
|       | 6.2   | Sub-dimension: Rules                                         | 66  |
|       |       | 6.2.1 Basic communication rules                              | 67  |
|       |       | 6.2.2 Flexible and explicit rules                            | 67  |
|       | 6.3   | Sub-dimension: Affiliation                                   | 68  |
|       |       | 6.3.1 Respect through attentive behavior                     | 69  |
|       |       | 6.3.2 Humor                                                  | 70  |
|       |       | 6.3.3 Openness                                               | 71  |
|       |       | 6.3.4 Friendliness                                           | 72  |
|       |       | 6.3.5 Encouragement                                          | 73  |
| 7     | Non-verbal behavior                                                  || 75  |
|       | 7.1   | Function of non-verbal behavior in lectures                  | 75  |
|       |       | 7.1.1 Facial expression                                      | 76  |
|       |       | 7.1.2 The gaze/the eye contact                               | 77  |
|       |       | 7.1.3 The posture                                            | 78  |
|       |       | 7.1.4 Spatial behavior (proxemics)                           | 79  |
|       |       | 7.1.5 Gestures                                               | 81  |
| 8     | Visualizations                                                       || 85  |
|       | 8.1   | Function of visualizations and illustrations                 | 85  |
|       |       | 8.1.1 Help with retention                                    | 86  |
|       |       | 8.1.2 Visualize                                              | 86  |
|       |       | 8.1.3 Organizing and structuring                             | 86  |
|       |       | 8.1.4 Arouse and influence motivation, emotions, attitudes, and interest | 86  |
|       |       | 8.1.5 Influencing decisions and behavior                     | 86  |
|       |       | 8.1.6 Indirect influence                                     | 86  |
|       |       | 8.1.7 Representation of concrete reality                     | 87  |
|       |       | 8.1.8 Truth function                                         | 87  |
|       | 8.2   | Types of diagrams                                            | 87  |
|       |       | 8.2.1 Process (linear or circular)                           | 87  |
|       |       | 8.2.2 Structure (hierarchy)                                  | 88  |
|       |       | 8.2.3 Ring                                                   | 89  |
|       |       | 8.2.4 Cluster                                                | 89  |
|       |       | 8.2.5 Rays                                                   | 90  |
|       | 8.3   | Diagrams as concepts                                         | 90  |
|       |       | 8.3.1 Process                                                | 91  |
|       |       | 8.3.2 Disclosure                                             | 91  |
|       |       | 8.3.3 Directions                                             | 91  |
|       |       | 8.3.4 Location                                               | 92  |
|       |       | 8.3.5 Influence                                              | 92  |

- 8.4 Dealing with data — 93
  - 8.4.1 Credibility — 93
  - 8.4.2 Meaning — 93
  - 8.4.3 Getting to the point — 93
  - 8.4.4 Selection — 93
- 8.5 Slide design — 93
  - 8.5.1 Aim of the lecture — 94
  - 8.5.2 Audience — 94
  - 8.5.3 Conciseness — 94
  - 8.5.4 Uniformity of the layout — 94
  - 8.5.5 Arrangement of the elements — 94
  - 8.5.6 Headings — 95
  - 8.5.7 Bullet points — 95
  - 8.5.8 Background — 95
  - 8.5.9 Standard templates — 95
  - 8.5.10 Pictures — 95
  - 8.5.11 Fonts with serifs — 96
  - 8.5.12 Font families and sizes — 96
  - 8.5.13 Accessibility — 96
  - 8.5.14 Branding — 96
  - 8.5.15 Copyright — 96

9 Teaching subject content through cooperative learning — 99
- 9.1 Cooperative learning and group performance — 99
  - 9.1.1 Process losses — 100
  - 9.1.2 Loss of coordination — 100
  - 9.1.3 Loss of motivation — 100
- 9.2 Areas for measures to reduce process losses — 101
  - 9.2.1 Management and monitoring — 101
  - 9.2.2 Work structure — 102
  - 9.2.3 Promoting cooperation by creating productive interdependencies (mutual dependency) — 103
- 9.3 Buzzgroups — 106
- 9.4 Problem-oriented, discovery-based learning — 108
- 9.5 Jigsaw ("group puzzle") — 112
- 9.6 Group tournament: Teams games tournament — 115
  - 9.6.1 Group work and online quizzes — 118
- 9.7 Case method — 119
- 9.8 Discussion — 122

|     |       |       | |
|-----|-------|-------|---|
|     | 9.8.1 | Definition | 122 |
|     | 9.8.2 | Target areas of discussion as a teaching method | 123 |
|     | 9.8.3 | General tasks of the discussion leader | 124 |
|     | 9.8.4 | Specific tasks and functions of the discussion leader | 124 |
| 9.9 | Model of direct instruction | | 130 |

## Part II Training program: Interactive and adaptive teaching of subject content

**10 Conceptual framework for interactive and adaptive teaching of subject content** — 133
- 10.1 Interactive lecturing — 133
- 10.2 Adaptive teaching — 134
    - 10.2.1 Macro level — 134
    - 10.2.2 Micro level — 136

**11 The training concept** — 139
- 11.1 The microteaching concept — 139
- 11.2 Components of a microteaching training program — 140
    - 11.1.1 The ability to use and analyze theoretical background knowledge — 141
    - 11.1.2 The ability to use conceptual structures of interaction processes for analysis and orientation — 141
    - 11.1.3 The ability to form hypotheses and make decisions — 142
    - 11.1.4 The ability to perform actions properly — 142
    - 11.1.5 Feedback in relation to specific effective skills — 143

**12 Effectiveness and appropriateness in the acquisition of behaviors and skills** — 145

**13 The selection of behavioral dimensions** — 147

**14 The contents of the training program** — 149
- 14.1 Dimension variation — 150
    - 14.1.1 Context factors for planning — 150
    - 14.1.2 Selection and combination of methods — 151
- 14.2 Dimension flexibility — 160
    - 14.2.1 Monitoring — 160
    - 14.2.2 Transitions — 160
    - 14.2.3 Relationship with individuals and the group — 162
- 14.3 Dimension evaluation — 164
    - 14.3.1 Assessment — 164
    - 14.3.2 Tests, examinations, and certificates of achievement — 164
    - 14.3.3 Feedback, praise, and recognition — 166

15 Results of the training program 169
   15.1 Results of the seminar evaluation questionnaire 169
   15.2 Results of the self- and alter competence questionnaire 170
   15.3 Summary 171

Bibliography 173
Index 181

# List of figures

Figure 1: Language conveys knowledge and culture — 4
Figure 2: The triangle represents the "authority to issue instructions" aspect under which this organizational chart can be described — 23
Figure 3: The triangle represents the "happiness or exchange" viewpoint from which the story can be told — 27
Figure 4: The triangle represents the "process quality" aspect under which the relationships in the network can be described — 28

# List of tables

| | | |
|---|---|---|
| Table 1: | Effect of teaching methods | 6 |
| Table 2: | Components for effective teaching and lecturing | 8 |
| Table 3: | Context factors | 9 |
| Table 4: | Context factors and their effects | 14 |
| Table 5: | Behavioral dimensions in the transfer of knowledge | 15 |
| Table 6: | Sub-dimension: Forms of organization | 19 |
| Table 7: | Sub-dimension: Basic structures | 22 |
| Table 8: | Skills for building a structure | 29 |
| Table 9: | Skills for classifying content | 31 |
| Table 10: | Skills to promote the absorption of information | 36 |
| Table 11: | Vagueness communication | 38 |
| Table 12: | Skills for all phases of the lecture | 40 |
| Table 13: | Skills for individual interest | 48 |
| Table 14: | Skills to create purposeful meaningful events | 51 |
| Table 15: | Classroom management skills (Lewis, 2023) | 52 |
| Table 16: | Technical systems to create targeted, meaningful events | 53 |
| Table 17: | Skills to create purposeful, meaningful events through verbal vividness | 55 |
| Table 18: | Enthusiasm during presentation | 59 |
| Table 19: | Skills for socially integrative presentation | 63 |

| | | |
|---|---|---:|
| Table 20: | Skills for Rules | 66 |
| Table 21: | Skills for socially effective interactions | 68 |
| Table 22: | Skills to show respect | 69 |
| Table 23: | Skills to show humor | 70 |
| Table 24: | Skills to show openness | 71 |
| Table 25: | Skills to show friendliness | 72 |
| Table 26: | Skills to show encouragement | 73 |
| Table 27: | Types of expression for non-verbal behavior | 76 |
| Table 28: | Functions of visualizations | 85 |
| Table 29: | Types of diagrams | 87 |
| Table 30: | Degree of interdependencies in the group work characteristics | 112 |
| Table 31: | Degree of interdependencies in the group work characteristics | 115 |
| Table 32: | Degree of interdependencies in the group work characteristics | 118 |
| Table 33: | Elements of a systematic microteaching training program | 132 |
| Table 34: | Microteaching training concept | 139 |
| Table 35: | Behavioral dimensions for training | 147 |
| Table 36: | Context factors | 150 |
| Table 37: | Results of the seminar evaluation questionnaire | 169 |
| Table 38: | Results of the self- and alter competence questionnaire | 170 |

# PART I
# EFFECTIVE COMMUNICATION AND PRESENTATION OF SUBJECT CONTENT

# CHAPTER 1

# Conceptual framework for the communication of knowledge and culture

## 1.1 Language as a unique social and cognitive skill

With language, humans have unique cognitive and social abilities and skills. We use language to organize social processes and to cope with the challenges and necessary adaptation processes to the environment. One of these processes is to cooperate in common actions. This includes the ability to pass on and impart cognitive and cultural knowledge. To impart knowledge, a shared intentionality is required (Tomasello, 2020). This means that two actors pursue a common goal and focus their attention on an object—that is, there is a two-level structure (Tomasello, 2020) that includes both commonality and individuality. The communication of information is therefore the cognitive ability to abstract, present an objective view of an entity, and communicate this using language. Therefore, it goes beyond one's own individual point of view.

These processes, which are only briefly described here, are important in classifying the processes that take place when conveying and imparting information and understanding what is ultimately at stake when conveying content. Presenting and communicating is always a cooperative process, with the common goal of knowing more and helping each other. You don't do it on your own. From an ontogenetic point of view, that wouldn't make sense either (Tomasello, 2020).

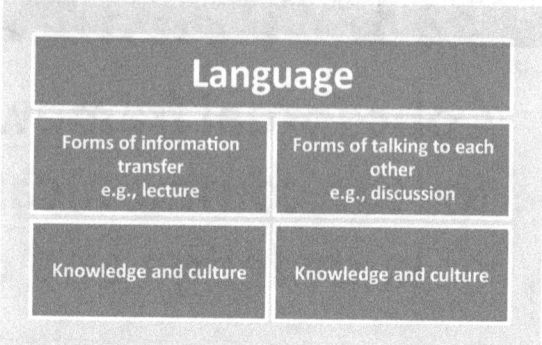

Figure 1: Language conveys knowledge and culture

In the course of human development, various forms of information transfer (lecture, presentation, instruction, lecture course) have been developed in many cultures, as well as an institutional collective framework and space. An institutional space is, for example, the university, where information is imparted with the help of lectures. In addition to the forms of imparting information, forms of talking to each other have also been developed, such as discussion, with the aim of deepening and consolidating content or acquiring further knowledge. However, a good discussion always involves imparting information.

Reliability is an essential element in the transfer of information. When an area of knowledge is introduced or expanded, the information must be trustworthy. It is interesting to note, for example, that children up to approximately 5–7 years old primarily trust the world knowledge of adults and not the knowledge they receive from their peers. Adults play a central role in imparting information about knowledge and culture. Without reliable information and the ability to change perspective (from I to you and we), there would have been no development of language from an ontogenetic perspective. Tomasello (2020) illustrated this perfectly with the example of hunting a deer: When I return to the campsite and inform the others in the group that there is a deer to hunt by the river, this information must be reliable; otherwise, my counterparts would not agree to follow my invitation a second time.

In the course of human history, very different methods of imparting knowledge and communicating specialist content have been developed.

## 1.2 Teaching methods for imparting knowledge

The question of what is considered a good and effective (communicative) method for imparting knowledge has been discussed for a very long time. Cicero (106–43 BC) dealt with the question of how best to teach in Rome at the time.

However, the question of "good" and the methods used to impart knowledge would be better replaced by questions such as "Good for which goals?," "Good for whom?," and "Good under which circumstances?" Interesting and valid knowledge on how to deal with these questions can be found in many specialist disciplines that deal with teaching.

If we agree with these questions and the views on which they are based (such as Joyce et al., 2014), then the search for the best, most effective, and most efficient knowledge transfer method is a questionable undertaking. Teaching methods are developed, shaped, or used on the basis of certain views of human nature and, as a result, certain types of learning objectives and procedures, as they are able to promote these views in each case. Therefore, they are only effective for what they were primarily developed for. In this way, certain goals are brought to the fore, and certain teaching approaches, teaching procedures or methods, and associated activities are selected and assigned to achieve them. By contrast, other goals and quite effective approaches are (sometimes necessarily) neglected (Joyce et al., 2014).

Example: If you believe that it is human nature to understand the world by acquiring knowledge, organizing it, sensing problems, and developing solutions for them, then you focus on the aspect of information processing. In this case, the lecture is a suitable method. Lectures aim to impart knowledge and are very effective in doing so (Klinzing, 1998). However, other goals of education and training, such as the development of social skills and independent learning, are neglected, if not prevented, by lectures.

Teaching methods are not just about achieving certain teaching effects. Teaching methods also have indirect effects, that is, educational effects and impacts that can also be achieved through their use. Direct effects relate to the mastery of certain learning materials and skills (e.g., the acquisition of knowledge and skills in the organization of knowledge within the framework of an academic discipline) and form the basis for teaching activities with the help of which they are to be mastered. They steer learners in certain directions. Indirect effects, by contrast, are conveyed through experiences with and within the teaching process and the learning environment it creates.

Example 1: The lecture, the presentation, and the instruction are, among other things, effective methods for imparting large amounts of knowledge. However, other effects (indirect effects) of education and training, such as the development of social skills and independent learning, are neglected, if not prevented.

Example 2: Competition between learners can stimulate the achievement of direct effects, but the atmosphere of a competitive situation can also antagonize learners (indirect effect).

Table 1: Effect of teaching methods

| Teaching method | Effect A: desirable? Effect B: desirable? Effect C: desirable? |
| --- | --- |

Thus, we have direct instructional effects and indirect or educational effects in teaching methods and in the transfer of knowledge. Therefore, when selecting procedures and teaching methods, they should be examined in terms of what effects they aim to achieve directly but also what effects they achieve indirectly. For example, a teaching method can also be selected because it has certain indirect "educational" effects, even if the direct objectives are not achieved as effectively.

### Exercise

Please summarize the basic idea of the previous argument.
Please design possible sensible combinations of teaching forms/methods you are familiar with:

## 1.3 Arguments for and against imparting knowledge in the form of lectures and presentations

Knowledge transfer in the form of lectures, presentations, or instructions is a procedure or method for imparting large amounts of knowledge and has several advantages, as shown below (cf. Bligh, 2000).

- Basic knowledge can be imparted quickly and reliably.
- Knowledge can be built up quickly and effectively.
- Up-to-date knowledge can be imparted quickly, flexibly, and directly.
- Own research results that are not (or not yet) available anywhere else can be communicated and shared.
- The aim is to successfully present connections that are not immediately recognizable to the audience.
- The audience can participate in the speaker's thought processes.
- One can reach hundreds of people with one lecture, and it is also a cost-effective format.
- A social event or situation is created that indirectly supports learning in many ways.

In addition to these advantages, there are also disadvantages. These include, for example, the following:

- There is a high degree of passivity.
- You cannot actively participate and think for yourself.
- The ability to remember is not particularly high, and a critical examination of the content is difficult.
- The advantages and disadvantages listed here are presented in this or a similar form by both supporters and opponents of monologic forms of communication.

Empirical studies (cf. Bligh, 2000; McKeachie, 1990), show that the method of lecturing is superior to other methods for imparting content that is needed in the short term for an application, as motivation for a topic, or as an introduction to a topic, whereas lecturing is inferior to other methods, such as discussion for long-term retention of information.

Another interesting result becomes clear when comparing traditional lectures with interactive lectures. Based on a meta-analysis of 225 empirical studies in STEM subjects in the USA, Freeman et al. (2014) showed that the performance of students in courses with interactive lectures was significantly better than courses with traditional lectures in terms of average exam results and that the probability of failing was 1.5 times higher in courses with traditional lectures. Very good results can also be seen in terms of retention performance when the subject content is taught interactively; this also increases student motivation. Interactive lectures combine and integrate additional methods to promote retention, interest, and motivation.

## 1.4 Integration of various components for effective lecturing and knowledge transfer

Effective teaching, instruction, and lecturing is a central part of a carefully constructed process consisting of various components that are coordinated and structured to ensure that

- knowledge is built up,
- knowledge is shared,
- learners are able to actively participate in this mediation process,
- reflection is encouraged,
- insights are provided into their own knowledge,

- the motivation to learn is created, and
- a productive learning environment is possible.

To achieve this, important components of lecturing, communicating, and instructing are integrated. For effective teaching, lecturing, and instruction, these components include planning and contextual factors, behavioral dimensions and the associated communicative skills, strategies to support learners, and collaborative methods.

Table 2: Components for effective teaching and lecturing

| Integration of elements for effective teaching and lecturing | Necessary for | Detailed in |
|---|---|---|
| Planning and context | Learning objectives<br>Audience<br>External conditions | Chapter 2: Planning and context factors for the preparation of lectures |
| Behavioral dimensions | Clarity and structure | Chapter 4: Clarity dimension |
| | Motivation and interest | Chapter 5: Motivation interest dimension |
| | Learning climate and atmosphere | Chapter 6: Social learning climate and social atmosphere |
| | Variation, flexibility and evaluation | Chapter 14: Contens of the training program |
| Communicative skills | Effectiveness and appropriateness | Chapters 3–14 |
| Non-verbal behavior | Effectiveness and appropriateness | Chapter 7: Non-verbal behavior |
| Support strategies | Visualization | Chapter 8: Visualization |
| Cooperative methods | Combination of lectures with cooperative methods | Chapter 9: Cooperative methods |

# CHAPTER 2

# Planning and contextual factors for the preparation of a lecture

Context factors must be taken into account when preparing lectures and presentations and include learning objectives, audience, and external circumstances. The type and manner of preparation depends on how detailed and how long certain content is presented.

Table 3: Context factors

| Contextual factors | Useful for |
|---|---|
| Learning objectives | Sustainability and motivation of learning |
| Audience | Consideration of the motives and background experience of those present |
| External conditions | Organization and planning |

## 2.1 Learning objectives

Creating and communicating learning objectives or lecture objectives is an important factor in effective teaching and lecturing. Clear learning objectives improve the sustainability of learning and motivation (Hattie, 2013). If you want your audience to be entertained by your lectures or presentation (which is legitimate) as well as help them learn something, the use of learning objectives is recommended. This is the first step in achieving sustainable and meaningful learning. Regardless of whether you are planning a seminar, a course, or just a teaching unit, effective teaching and the resulting learning require clearly defined objectives.

To determine learning objectives, Bloom et al. (1956) developed taxonomies for learning objectives in the cognitive, affective, and psychomotor areas. These taxonomies of learning objectives have been and continue to be used successfully worldwide and are considered among the best-known taxonomies in the field of learning objectives. Learning objectives help us plan and reflect on what we want to achieve in terms of content.

Another well-known approach to formulating goals for teaching was developed by Robert Mager (1975). His perspective is action-oriented and specific in terms of behavioral objectives. The objectives describe the behavior, the conditions, and the evaluation criteria for the behavior exhibited.

## 2.1.1 Specific learning objectives

In addition to the general objectives that need to be considered in a lecture, such as conveying general knowledge or an overview of a topic, specific objectives are also helpful and often necessary when conveying specialist content and knowledge.

An objective describes the different levels of what learners need to know or be able to do. If these objectives are missing, it is difficult to determine the effectiveness of the mediation or teaching. If no learning objectives are formulated, there is, therefore, no secure basis for selecting further methods to deepen the content. Thus, it is important that you have a clear idea of what the learners should know and be able to do at the end of the lecture or lesson. By clearly describing learning objectives, you can, for example, include tests to determine learning success.

The procedure described below is suitable for describing the desired behavior:

- Name the characteristics and type of behavior as well as the characteristics of learning success so that the learner achieves the goal.
- Try to determine the desired behavior and the characteristics of the learning success more precisely by identifying its most important prerequisites.
- As a benchmark for the desired behavior, indicate how well the behavior must be expressed to be considered satisfactory.

A learning objective is one that has the above-mentioned characteristics—that is, the behavior you are aiming for is clearly formulated.

## 2.1.2 Steps for determining learning objectives

The description of the learning objective should show what the learner needs to do to demonstrate that the objective has been achieved. Since we cannot guess what others are thinking, we must rely on observing behavior and performance to determine the level of understanding and scope of skills. However, we can ask them to answer questions orally or in writing or to demonstrate certain skills. Therefore, lecturers must clearly determine the type of behavior and the characteristics of learning success.

Below are three examples of how general learning objectives can be described more precisely by specific objectives.

1. *General learning objective:* You want learners to understand how a heat pump works.
   A specific goal would be: "After the instruction or lesson, learners must be able to name and explain the three operating principles of the heat pump."
2. *General learning objective:* You want learners to know how batteries can be recycled using online journals to find relevant information.
   A specific goal would be: "With the help of the three most important international specialist journals, learners should become familiar with at least five processes that can be used to recycle batteries."
3. *General learning objective:* You want learners to understand the ideas and characteristics of the Enlightenment.
   A specific goal would be: "Choose a text from Lessing's 'Nathan the Wise' and describe which values the three characters you have chosen embody in this play and how this affects their treatment of others. Then, discuss your findings in the group."

---

### EXERCISE

Formulate a specific learning objective for the general learning objective "Apply quadratic equations."

---

## 2.2 Target audience

When preparing and planning a lecture or presentation, it is also important to consider the target audience. The following questions are important:

What are the motives for participating?

The motives for attending an event are not always immediately clear at the outset. The motives range from voluntary participation and pure interest in the topic to mandatory participation to obtain approval for an examination or thesis or because an employer wants participation in a particular continuing education topic or field of knowledge.

What is the background experience of the audience?

A common background in terms of age, education, and preferences often enables better and easier access to the target group. This is particularly important when using examples. If there is a common background of experience, examples can be used more effectively and in a more targeted manner. If this common background of experience is not available, examples, comparisons, and scenarios must be selected very carefully so that they do not confuse or irritate the audience.

What do the audience know?

This is the most difficult question to answer. If it is an ongoing course that extends over several weeks or months, it is possible to discover more about the level of knowledge of the audience as the course progresses. If, on the other hand, it is a one-off event, you often do not have the opportunity to determine the level of knowledge of the audience. A good option is to give a general overview of the topic in the form of a hierarchy at the beginning of the lecture or presentation, and then explicitly highlight the area that you want to go into in more detail in your lecture. In this way, the overall context of a topic area can be presented quickly and effectively. You will remind those who are already familiar with the topic and provide a clear structure for those who are new to the topic by highlighting the key points that you will focus on in this lecture.

What is the reason for this event?

Was I invited, or did I invite myself to this event? Was I only invited because no one else was available? Am I working on behalf of a third party, am I representing a company/institution or am I just representing myself? In what context is the event taking place? Are formal requirements placed on me? What is the atmosphere like? Are the audience dismissive, approving, or cautious? Are there problems in this company or group that I should solve? Try to get a clear picture of the reason for the event with the help of the questions.

## 2.3 External conditions

Group size plays an important role in choosing the technique, exercises, and interaction with the group. The larger the group, the more difficult it is to present the content interactively.

The size of the room also influences your own behavior. In large rooms, people use more gestures and change position, thus creating more interest and attention. Clean rooms have a positive influence on the processing of information. Cold rooms (temperature) lead to discomfort and impair the ability to process information.

Time frame also plays a role. Make sure you stick to the time limit. If the previous speakers have not kept to the time limit, you may only have 15 minutes for your lecture or presentation instead of 30 minutes. Therefore, if it is a very important lecture or presentation, prepare yourself to be able to give the lecture in half the time.

Further, prepare the media in such a way that the lecture is also available on another medium and can therefore be transferred to another medium easily and without great delay.

The Table 4 shows that the context factors of learning objective, audience, and external circumstances, as well as the choice of learning methods, have an impact on the selection, weighting, and sequence of the information in the lecture or presentation. Presenters are always responsible for this weighting. These contextual factors are important and must be taken into account during planning and preparation.

Table 4: Context factors and their effects

| Contextual factors | Effects for all context factors in relation to |
|---|---|
| Learning objectives<br>• General<br>• Specific | Selection of information |
| Audience<br>• Level of knowledge<br>• Background experience<br>• Atmosphere | Weighting of information |
| External conditions<br>• Group size<br>• Room size<br>• Duration | Order of information |
| Teaching methods<br>• Lecturing/presentation<br>• Group work<br>• Discussion | Weighting of social interaction |

# CHAPTER 3

# Behavioral dimensions in imparting knowledge

Another important question is how to arrive at the factors and components that are important for the transfer of knowledge.

To develop and select the *main components* that are important for conveying content and knowledge in the form of a subject-specific lecture or presentation (monologue forms), it is crucial to first define the *essential behavioral dimensions*. *Effective skills* are then assigned to these.

Table 5: Behavioral dimensions in the transfer of knowledge

| Behavioral dimensions | Useful for |
|---|---|
| Clarity and structure | Forms of organization<br>Basic structures |
| Motivation and interest | Individual interest<br>Situational interest |
| Social learning climate and social atmosphere | Control<br>Rules<br>Affiliation |

*Behavioral dimensions* can be used as criteria for evaluating and categorizing interactions (Argyle, 2017; Rupp, 2019) and take place constantly and automatically in daily communication. The following example illustrates this.

If you are asked the question after a lecture: "How was the lecture you just listened to?," one answer could be: "Very good, the lecture was clear, understandable, and interesting." The answer "very good …" is thus given at a general, highly abstract level. This helps us get a first impression, and the answer reflects two dimensions of behavior or perception: clarity and attention. However, the answer will usually not include specific, concrete *behaviors to* get a better idea of what exactly was rated as "very good" in this talk. So, for example, "The speaker specifically used transitions and repetitions to create a clear structure." *Behavioral dimensions* are therefore the starting point for the development of specific *skills*, which in turn can be used to present and convey subject-specific lecture content effectively.

The following behavioral dimensions are of great importance for the perception and effectiveness of subject lectures or presentations and are the basis for the following explanations:

- Creating clarity for the structure, outline, and structure of a specialist lecture/presentation and instruction
- Generating motivation and attention from the audience during a lecture/presentation or instruction
- Creating a conducive learning atmosphere during a subject-specific lecture, presentation, or instruction

Behavioral dimensions thus provide a direction for action and make it possible to identify and operationalize effective (target) behaviors/skills that in turn support these dimensions. The effective and appropriate use of such (target) behaviors leads to the audience's perception (feeling) that "the lecture was clearly structured, it was interesting, and I felt comfortable." Target behaviors/skills are important to practice in a training session.

The components and behavioral dimensions of effective lecturing, presenting, instructing, and teaching subject content selected for this book relate to the most important dimensions and factors for effective knowledge transfer and excellent teaching found in research over the past 50 years and are presented in each chapter with the associated skills. These include the components of planning (Woolfolk, 2014), learning objectives (Bloom et al., 1956), and the dimensions of "clarity" (Bligh, 2000; Gage & Berliner, 1996; Jameson Boex, 2000; Klinzing, 1998); "structuring" (Bligh, 2000; Barkley & Mayor, 2018); structure (Gage & Berliner, 1996; Klinzing, 1998); interest (Klinzing, 1998); "enthusiasm and engagement"

(Reyes-Fournier et al., 2020); "knowledgeable, creative and enthusiasm" (Buskist & Kelley, 2018); "enthusiasm and interest" (Barkley & Mayor, 2018); social climate (Klinzing, 1998); control & affiliation (Brekelmans et al., 2011; Rupp, 1998); and "respect" (Kelley et al., 2016).

The dimensions mentioned above complement each other perfectly but can also be in conflict with each other. If the lecture or presentation focuses only on clarity and structure, the other dimensions will be neglected. If you only want to arouse interest and motivation, clarity and structure will be neglected. If the focus is only on a pleasant atmosphere, structure, interest, and motivation will be lacking. It is crucial to find the right balance between these dimensions to convey specialist content effectively and appropriately. Depending on the situation, it may nevertheless be necessary to emphasize and consider one dimension more strongly, focusing on that dimension for a longer period of time to achieve a specific goal when presenting. By combining the dimensions in your lecture or presentation, you create an environment in which your audience can better understand the content, take an interest in the topic and actively participate in the mutual exchange.

Now, we just need the communication skills to implement these dimensions effectively and appropriately.

## 3.1 The effectiveness and appropriateness of communicative skills

Effectiveness and appropriateness are two important characteristics of acquiring communicative skills for interaction processes and interaction-intensive situations, as they are constantly required during lectures and in class.

Effectiveness is defined for skills in such a way that it is possible to describe whether a skill is suitable for achieving a goal. For example, I need communicative skills for a presentation to emphasize a point. On a verbal level, this can be implemented with the phrase, "This point is particularly important." On a nonverbal level, this can also be emphasized by raising your voice. Using this skill is also a structure-promoting measure.

These effective skills are presented in detail in the respective chapters that describe the behavioral dimensions. The use of such effective skills measurably improves the quality of instruction, lecture, or presentation.

However, effectiveness is not the only factor to consider when using skills. The appropriateness of use is also of crucial importance.

Appropriateness means using the right skills to the right extent, at the right time, in the right way, and for the right purpose. Appropriateness means being able to cope with many different situations.

For example, to point out the importance of certain information in a lecture, this can be done, as described above, in the form of a verbal signal, such as, "This point is particularly important." The speaker points out the importance of the point by using the word "important." Pointing out the importance of a point is a very effective communicative behavior in terms of the listener's retention performance. However, if the speaker uses this behavior in every single sentence, it can become inappropriate.

Appropriateness also includes the ability to comply with and respect the norms that apply to a situation in an encounter. However, this also includes the possibility of failing in a communicative interaction, and the people with whom one interacts should show tolerance toward inappropriate behavior when using individual skills. When developing our communicative skills, we need a large number and variety of different situations. It is crucial that we learn from the use of inappropriate behavior. To change a behavior, we need to be made aware of it, and we need effective target behaviors that help us to develop and change in this direction and, as a result, to act effectively and appropriately.

If we have such effective target skills at our disposal, we can use them in a wide variety of communicative situations. Effective communication skills are essential for success. Based on this concept and these fundamental considerations, the important dimensions of perception and the associated skills that are important for imparting knowledge during a lecture, presentation, instruction, or when applying a teaching method are described below.

# CHAPTER 4

# Behavioral dimension: Clarity

The behavioral dimension of clarity includes the sub-dimensions of forms of organization and basic structures. The following sections, therefore, deal with forms of organization and basic structures for building, organizing, and structuring a subject lecture or presentation. This is usually done during preparation. However, it is also possible to incorporate other structuring elements during the lecture or presentation.

A clear, comprehensible structure and organization of the lecture is an essential feature and a good prerequisite for the lecture to be understandable and memorable. Decisive for the comprehensibility and memorability of a lecture are the external and internal structures (forms of organization), as well as a clear basic structure in the form of hierarchy, sequential structure, or network (Bligh, 2000; Gage & Berliner, 1996; Klinzing, 1998).

## 4.1 Sub-dimension: Forms of organization

Table 6: Sub-dimension: Forms of organization

| Forms of organization | Useful for |
| --- | --- |
| External structure | Formal structure<br>Comprehensibility |
| Internal structure | Consistency of thought<br>Memorability |

## 4.1.1 External structure of a lecture through formal outline features

An *external content structure* of lectures is achieved through formal structure features. A visualization shows the structure of the lecture. Scientific lectures or presentations in particular, similar to research reports and specialist texts, are characterized by a high degree of formal structure.

1. *Structure with letters and numbers (alphanumeric structure)*
    Part A: Latin capital letters
        Chapter I: Roman numerals
            1. Arabic numerals
                a. Latin lowercase letters
                    α. Greek lowercase letters
2. *Structure with numbers*

    1.
    1.1
    1.1.1
    2.
    2.1
    2.1.1

Example: Four-level hierarchy linking the two systems. A fifth level can easily be introduced.

   A Introduction
      I Problem
   B Objectives
      II General objectives
         1. Overview
         2. Target level
            2.1 Basics
            2.2 The target system

An outline at the first or second level is sufficient for an overview at the beginning of a lecture. Further hierarchies and bullet points can then be added as the lecture progresses.

Positive example with one level:

1. Albert Bandura
2. The triadic–reciprocal model
3. Processes of a self-regulating system

Positive example with a second level:

1. Albert Bandura
2. The triadic–reciprocal model
    2.1. Self-control
    2.2. Self-regulation
    2.3. Self-efficacy
3. Processes of a self-regulating system

For the external outline, it is important that the structure of the lecture or presentation is made visible in the form of a visualization. Verbal and non-verbal behaviors help to support the structure of the lecture. On the verbal level, this includes the following behaviors:

- Preliminary and interim remarks, for example, "Let me move on to the next point." or "I now come to point three."
- A clear indication of what is particularly important, for example, "Point two, self-efficacy in Albert Bandura's triadic-reciprocal model, is particularly important."

Further skills to promote and support organization and structure are described in detail in Section 4.3.

## 4.1.2 Internal structure of a lecture through consistency

In addition to the external structure, which can be presented effectively in the form of a visualization, an internal structure is also important in the lecture. This should express that the sentences are related to each other and not simply strung together and that there is no compelling logic in what is said. It is also important to ensure that the individual points are not just read out without providing a transition to the next main point. The information presented within a main point must, in turn, be presented and recited in a meaningful order. This is because too many breaks in thought are not appreciated and lead to confusion with regard to the content presented.

## 4.2 Sub-dimension: Basic structures

Table 7: Sub-dimension: Basic structures

| Basic structures | Useful for |
|---|---|
| Hierarchy | Organization of knowledge |
| Sequential structure | Representation of linear processes<br>Sequence of events |
| Network | Establishing relationships between concepts and content |

Thus, it is important that a lecture has a clear objective, is well structured, and follows a certain logic, thus enabling meaningful learning.

Ausubel's (1974) theory of meaningful learning assumes that meaningful learning involves the "acquisition of meanings." Three conditions must be met for meaningful learning to take place: The newly presented information must be clear and relate to the learners' existing knowledge. The learners have prior knowledge that is relevant to the new information. Detailed knowledge of a specific subject should be acquired.

A good and effective way to achieve this is to organize a lecture using basic structures. These basic structures include:

1. the hierarchy,
2. the sequential structure, and
3. the network.

### 4.2.1 Hierarchical structure

Knowledge can be organized very well in a hierarchical structure, and we can find many examples of this in everyday life and in the respective specialist disciplines. The contents or concepts are summarized under a certain uniform aspect. This also includes well-known classification systems, such as the periodic table in chemistry: the periodic table is a list of all chemical elements ordered by increasing the nuclear charge. In biology, relationships between organisms are often presented in the form of diagrams or family trees. In business administration, an organizational chart is a good way to show the organizational hierarchy. An organizational chart can show the authority of the respective levels or the respective persons responsible for a level or department.

Hierarchies are of great value for effective learning, as they help organize and structure knowledge, even if the structure still has to be built up over time from small sections of interconnected ideas and statements. This process allows knowledge to be applied in different contexts and increases retention. In addition, many research findings (Anderson, 2013) show that the brain likes to organize information hierarchically.

The hierarchy is a frequently chosen form for presenting content, whereby the point of view or perspective from which the hierarchy is established must also be mentioned.

A. Applying the structure

# Example: Organizational Chart

The following example shows an organizational chart with four hierarchy levels. The triangle represents the perspective from which the organizational chart is described. In this example, the triangle represents the "authority to issue instructions" perspective. However, a different perspective can also be selected. For example, the organizational chart can be used to show which department is particularly effective or which department urgent process needs improvement.

The hierarchy levels must also be taken into account. Many people jump from one hierarchical level to the next when presenting without indicating this with verbal signals. It must always be clear which hierarchy level the presenter is

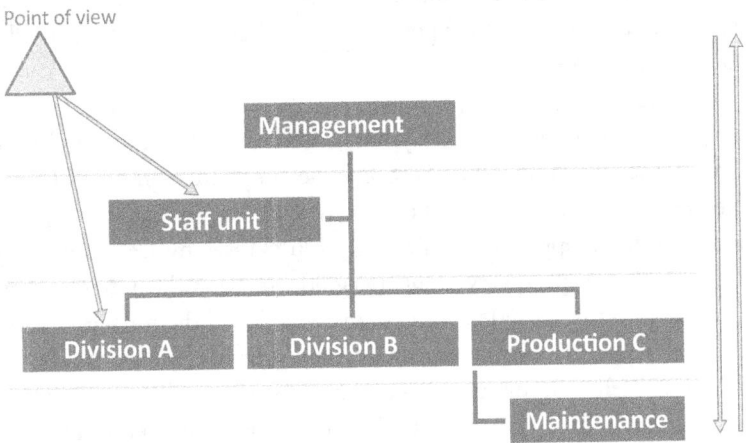

Figure 2: The triangle represents the "authority to issue instructions" aspect under which this organizational chart can be described

currently on. For example, you can present a hierarchy and then start directly with one of the visualized points. With a hierarchy, you show the overall context of a topic, show where the topic or point is classified in the overall context, and then explain this point directly.

### B. Point of view

In the hierarchy, the point of view or perspective (visualized by the triangle) from which the hierarchy is displayed is important. One perspective from which this hierarchy can be presented is, for example, the authority to issue instructions.

### 4.2.2 Linear sequential structure

To explain a point itself, another basic structure is required: a linear, sequential structure. This structure is illustrated in the next example using the fairy tale "Hans in Luck" by the Brothers Grimm.

### A. Applying the structure

## Example: Hans in Luck

Hans had served his master for seven years when he said to him, "Lord, my time is up. Now I would like to go home to my mother, give me my wages." The master replied, "You have served me faithfully and honestly, as your service has been, so shall your reward be," and gave him a piece of gold as big as Hans' head. Hans pulled his handkerchief out of his pocket, wrapped put the lump on his shoulder, and made his way home.

As he walked along, always putting one leg in front of the other, a rider came into his sight, trotting past on a lively horse, fresh and cheerful. "Oh," said Hans loudly, "what a lovely thing riding is! Someone sits there as if on a chair, doesn't bump into a stone, saves his shoes, and gets away. He doesn't know how." The rider, who had heard this, stopped, and called out, "Oh Hans, why are you walking too?" "I have to. I have a lump to carry home. It's gold, but I can't keep my head straight, and it's pressing on my shoulder." "You know what," said the horseman. "We want to swap. I'll give you my horse, and you give me your lump." "With all my heart," said Hans, "but I tell you, you must drag yourselves with it." The rider dismounted, took the gold, and helped Hans up, gave him the reins firmly in his hands and said, "If you want to go quickly, you must click your tongue and shout 'hop hop hop.'"

Hans was so happy when he sat on the horse and rode along so freely. After a while, it occurred to him that he should go even faster, and he began to click his tongue and shout "chop chop." The horse set off at a strong trot, and before Hans knew it, he was thrown off and lying in a ditch that separated the fields from the country road. The horse would have gone through if it had not been stopped by a farmer who had come along the road driving a cow in front of him. Hans gathered his limbs and got back on his feet. But he was vexed, and said to the farmer, "It is bad fun to ride, especially when you come upon such a cow as this, which knocks you and throws you down so that you may break your neck, and I will never sit up again. I praise your cow. Someone can walk behind it with ease, and on top of that is sure of his milk, butter, and cheese every day. What I would give to have a cow like that!" "Well," said the farmer, "if it is such a great favor to you, I will exchange the cow for the horse." Hans agreed with a thousand joys. The farmer swung himself onto his horse and rode off in a hurry.

… Then he drove his cow on, always toward his mother's village. The heat became more oppressive as midday approached, and Hans found himself in a heat that must have lasted another hour. He became so hot that his tongue stuck to the roof of his mouth from thirst. "… Listen, Hans," said the butcher, "For your sake, I will swap and leave you the pig for the cow."

"God reward you for your friendship!" said Hans, handing him the cow and letting him untie the piglet from the cart and give him the rope it was tied to. …

He was then joined by a fellow who carried a beautiful white goose under his arm. … Good Hans was afraid. "Oh, God," said he, "help me out of this trouble, you know better around here." Take my pig there and let me have your goose. "I must risk something," replied the lad, "but I don't want to be to blame for your misfortune." So he took the rope in his hand and quickly drove the pig away along a by-path; but good Hans, relieved of his cares, went home with the goose under his arm.

… When he had passed through the last village, there stood a scissors-grinder with his cart: … "How can you still ask," answered Hans. "I am becoming the happiest man on earth: I have money, as often as I reach into my pocket. What need I worry any longer?" He handed him the goose and took the whetstone.

… Then he sat down, and was about to stoop to drink when he made a mistake, bumped a little, and both stones went tumbling down. Hans, when he had seen them sink into the depths with his eyes, jumped up for joy, and then kneeled down and thanked God with tears in his eyes that he had shown him this mercy, and had delivered him from the heavy stones in such a good way, and without his having to reproach himself: the only thing that would have hindered him was that.

"There is no man under the sun so happy as I am," he exclaimed. With a light heart and free of all burdens, he skipped away until he was home with his mother.

Excerpt from KHM 83 Source: https://khm.li/Impressum

In this fairy tale "Hans in Luck" by the Brothers Grimm, we have a linear, sequential structure. This means that one point follows another. Hans gets gold, ... then a horse, ... then a cow, ... then a pig, ... then a goose, ... then a grindstone, and finally happiness. You can't go far wrong when telling the story in this order. However, the individual structural points can be embellished to varying degrees.

Gold: The gold is as big as Hans' head. The gold is wrapped in a cloth. The cloth belongs to Hans, who has received it from a friend, and it is also very valuable to him. He puts the gold on his shoulder ... These points can be further embellished and, if necessary, provided with additional information. For example, what was the value of gold at the time? What could you buy for its equivalent value? Thus, the individual points can be embellished and supplemented in very different ways.

In many scientific or engineering subjects and fields of knowledge, a linear structure is often predetermined. For example, the process of a production unit can always be represented by a sequence of steps. However, one problem that often arises with the speaker is the attention to detail. Every sub-step or every point within a process is explained in great detail. However, this often means that those listening, especially if they are not yet very familiar with a topic area, lose sight of the overall process and come into conflict with the interestingness.

Even in the fairy tale of Hans in Luck, not all points need to be explained in detail. Depending on our goal, the audience, and the time, we may have to make a choice regarding which point we want to dwell on longer and give a more detailed description. In concrete terms, this means that I can describe the gold or the goose, for example, in more detail and only briefly mention other points, such as the horse and the cow.

By presenting the overall structure, we create a general overview of the topic. But then I select just one point, which I describe, analyze, and explain in detail in my lecture.

## B. Point of view

The point of view or perspective (visualized by the triangle) on which this story or fairy tale is based is also important in the sequential linear structure.

Figure 3: The triangle represents the "happiness or exchange" viewpoint from which the story can be told

One perspective from which this story can be told, for example, is barter. The exchange takes place from the gold to the horse to the grinding stone. Afterward, Hans seems to have made a bad deal with every exchange. But if you take „happiness" as the perspective, a completely new way of telling the fairy tale emerges. The message here is, "Happiness grows by valuing experiences over possessions." With this fairy tale, you can point out the great importance of happiness in life. The most important thing in life is the happiness of going home and seeing your mother again. Told at the time, it makes another important statement. It is a so-called classic "poor people's tale." What could you achieve back then? Is it really possible to become rich through seven years of hard work? Isn't it better to be free of all burdens and see your mother again with a light heart?

When presenting specialist knowledge, there are, therefore, many possibilities if we choose a clear structure, determine the details that are important to us and that we want to deepen, and choose a point of view from which the individual structural points are explained.

### 4.2.3 Network structure

If the goal is to show the relationships between individual points, such as concepts or facts, this can be implemented in the form of a network. This representation not only explains the concepts or facts in isolation from each other but also addresses the relationship between the individual concepts or facts. A network therefore describes the quality of the relationships between individual points.

A. Applying the structure

# Example: Quality criteria

To illustrate a network, the quality criteria for a product are chosen as an example. They are all interconnected and form a network. The figure shows the connections between the individual criteria. The network is described under the aspect of "process quality."

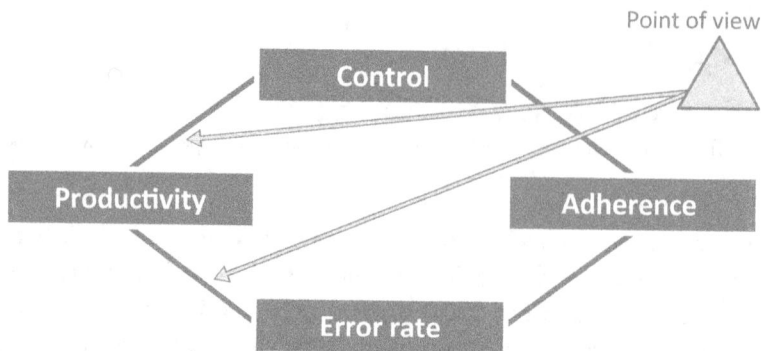

Figure 4: The triangle represents the "process quality" aspect under which the relationships in the network can be described

### B. Point of view

The illustration shows quality criteria from the perspective of process quality. Here, however, the adherence to delivery dates and their process quality, as well as the relationship between the two points, is selected, and this is explained from the selected point of view. In other words, the adherence to deadlines or the error rate is not described in isolation; it is integrated with the process quality of the relationship between adherence to deadlines and the error rate from the point of view of process quality. Once again, a visualization helps the speakers present a network, structure the topic, and make the relationships clear.

## 4.3 The clarity of execution

The previous chapter described the two sub-dimensions of *forms of organization* and *basic structures of the behavioral dimension of clarity*, which can *form the basis of* a technical lecture, a presentation, or an instruction. With the help of these basic structures, such a lecture can be clearly structured, organized, and structured. This is done during preparation.

However, further *measures and skills* are also necessary *during the lecture* to support the prepared outline and make the lecture or instruction clear, understandable, and memorable.

This chapter covers *skills* that promote and improve the *clarity of execution*. This includes skills that

- make it easier for the listener to think and understand the new content and create a clear structure,
- promote the integration of new information into existing knowledge and thus memorization, and
- facilitate the absorption of information through the clarity of speech.

These skills can be used for explanations, instructions, short or long statements/instructions, spontaneous answers to questions, and all dialogic communicative situations in which it is necessary to convey introductory or further information. The only decisive criterion is that information "flows"—that is, it is passed on.

Other measures and skills that make the lecture *interactive* and thus promote interest, attention, and memorability are described in the chapter "Motivation and interest."

## 4.3.1 Skills that promote the development of a clear structure at the beginning of a lecture

Table 8: Skills for building a structure

| Skills | Useful for |
| --- | --- |
| Content overview | Emphasize train of thought |
| Methodological overview | Show the procedure |
| Goals and topic | Creating a frame of reference |

As shown above, a lecture or presentation should be structured around the main ideas. These main ideas provide a framework on which the details and further information are developed, established, and organized. If you convey these main ideas—the structure—the audience will always know where you are. In this way, you encourage active thinking, categorization into a different body of knowledge, and retention.

To support this, you can use the following skills at the beginning, during, and at the end of a lecture:

### A. Provide an overview of the content

The brief description of the most important content of a lecture, the highlighting and disclosure of the outline, provides a focus for those present (Chilcoat, 1987). It draws attention to the presentation's train of thought, its main points, and how they are linked. Such an overview enables the audience to differentiate between main topics and explanatory details from the outset and thus to think along better. It also serves to pre-structure the content. The overview can be presented on the blackboard, on the flipchart, using a PowerPoint presentation, or in documents handed out.

## B. Provide a methodological overview

In addition to the content points given in an overview, in an interactive presentation, it is also important to point out the methods used in these interaction processes. By explaining at the beginning of the presentation what will happen methodically, everyone is included in the overall process, trust is created, the atmosphere is improved, and the dominance of the presenter is reduced.

Example: "Today, we are going to look at the topic 'Ontogenesis of communication.' The central points x, y, z will be presented. There will be a break after each central point, during which you will have the opportunity to discuss the content in depth in groups of 3 for about 10 minutes and then discuss the results in plenary. As we go along, I will explain the exact requirements for the individual activities once again. Are there any questions about this procedure?"

## C. Specify goals and topic

Communicating the objectives—that is, what the audience should take away from the presentation and what they need to be able to do afterward—and naming the topic and content also give the audience a frame of reference, a focus that makes it easier for them to actively think about and link the new material with their existing knowledge. Naming the objective and the topic therefore has the function of preparing the audience for what you want to say and has a structure-building and linking effect.

Example: "The topic of today's lecture is individual communication skills for a presentation. The aim of the lecture is for you to get to know the individual skills and the importance of effectiveness and appropriateness in terms of behavior."

However, phrases such as "You know what today is about" or "Who knows what topic is being discussed today?" are often used at the beginning of a lecture. Surely everyone knows what the most important points in the upcoming lecture will be, and the topic is also known. Therefore, these phrases are not helpful for the introduction. Instead, there is a simpler and more effective way: state the objectives and topic of the lecture and give an overview of what you intend to do.

However, it may not always be right, and can even lead to boredom, to always state the objectives and topic at the beginning. Therefore, if you first want to arouse interest in and attention to a topic, you should choose a different start and introduction. For example, a scenario or a case can be presented.

### 4.3.2 Skills that promote thinking and understanding of the content during a lecture

Table 9: Skills for classifying content

| Skills | Useful for |
|---|---|
| Meaning clues | Emphasize points |
| Transition signals | Clarify the train of thought |
| Interim summary | Structuring and memorizing |
| Examples | Using the background of experience |
| Rule-example-rule technique | Integration of knowledge |
| Scenario/case study | Clarify facts |
| Analogy | Show connections |
| Comparison | Understanding |
| Metaphor | Transfer context |

#### A. Use of meaning clues/importance clues

Meaning clues help to emphasize the important points in the lecture, and they enable a gradation according to importance, an evaluation. Significance clues emphasize particularly important statements or terms and inform the audience that they should pay particular attention (Chilcoat, 1987).

There are three groups of meaning clues:

1. *Verbal and non-verbal highlighting skills:* Verbal cues draw attention to the fact that a particularly important information, term, or concept is about to be presented.

   Example: "Pay particular attention to the following context." "This point is particularly important." "Very important in this context is …" These verbal indications of meaning can also be accompanied by reasons.
   Example: "This concept is very important for understanding xy."

   The verbal cue is given non-verbally by changing the volume and pitch of the voice (the more important, the louder and higher the pitch), by making a specific pause before an important point, by making illustrative gestures,

by changing the body posture, and by facial expressions (accentuation by frowning and raising the eyebrows).
2. *Enumeration:* It is also possible to emphasize something important by using enumerations before the exact content. For example, "There are three important groups of meaning clues, first ..., second ..., third ..." This list can be supported by gestures.
3. *Use repetitions in a targeted manner:* Targeted repetition can also be used to emphasize important information and terms. This is particularly useful when new, unfamiliar terms are introduced in the lecture or presentation. This targeted repetition takes place immediately after the first mention of the new thought, term, etc., and is formulated as a separate sentence. However, targeted repetitions can also be used in other sections of the lecture to improve the memorability of important terms and information.

## B. Use of transition signals

A good structure—that is, a good outline of the instruction or presentation—is a good help in understanding the speaker's train of thought (Chilcoat, 1987). However, having a good structure alone is not sufficient; it should also be repeatedly revealed and clarified to the audience during the lecture.

This is done, for example, by clearly demarcating sections of the lecture with transition signals, such that the listener recognizes that, for example, the speaker has now finished this section and a new one is about to begin. Such transition signals are verbal or non-verbal cues or formulations that appear at the end or beginning of a section of the lecture and make it clear to the listener that one section has now ended and the next is about to begin.

Example: "So far I have described bibliography, in the next part, the second part of my article, I will provide information on how to excerpt specialist literature, that is, how to record basic information from a text."

Possible formulations are also, for example: "I will now move on to the next section"; in the second part I will ... "If you have given an overview of the structure of your lecture or presentation at the beginning of your lecture and have shown this in writing on the blackboard, flipchart, or with the help of a PowerPoint presentation, you can use these visualizations as an additional structure-building measure for section boundaries. This also clarifies where you are in the outline."

Verbal transition techniques can also be combined effectively with non-verbal transition techniques. Non-verbal signals can be: a clear lowering of the voice at the end of a section, combined with eye contact; a short pause in speaking for about two seconds; lowering the gaze, for example, to the manuscript, followed by a clear restart with a slightly louder voice, combined with a resumption of eye contact with the audience; an upright posture combined with a slight turn to the left or right toward the audience; or a facial expression that shows a friendly smile and supports the transition.

## C. Use of interim summaries

Summaries are made at important sections or transitions during the lecture and present the important thoughts and the core of the information again in brief form. Interim summaries have three functions. First, they are an important marker of an outline; they help you to think along and thus offer another way of structuring. Second, by repeating the important ideas, they promote the retention of the content, the new content can be better integrated into existing knowledge. Third, as with the summary at the end of a lecture, they can be used to focus on specific points in order to draw attention to the main ideas of the information presented or to recall or reveal the structure and perspective used so far.

Example: "We have now covered two essential points in academic writing, bibliography and excerpting. The important thing about these two points is that they help us to lay a foundation for our further work and that they increase the likelihood that we will be able to clearly distinguish between our own and others' thoughts."

## D. Use of examples

Examples are explanations of something general, an individual case, a concept, rules, or laws. Examples are suitable for relating information and concepts that are still unknown to the existing knowledge and background experience of the audience. This is particularly effective if the audience's background of experience/knowledge is known and the examples are (or can be) selected accordingly (Chilcoat, 1987).

However, this is not always as easy as it sounds, because with a heterogeneous audience, there is often no common background of experience. The older the speakers and the younger the audience, the more different the culture of the speakers as opposed to the audience; the more different the composition of the audience, the more difficult it is to find suitable examples. Technologies, films, and music that were well-known and popular 20 or 30 years ago can astonish a young audience because they lack a common background of experience. However, new terms and information are remembered particularly well if they are linked to the knowledge and background of the audience. Such a link with existing knowledge is known as elaboration. If this is possible, the depth of processing of the information can be improved, what has been learned can be related to other memory content, and the probability of remembering can be increased.

Caution is advised if only one example is used to build up the entire lecture or presentation. As a rule, this cannot be sustained because there are too many exceptions, and the example may no longer serve its purpose or be used accordingly. The same applies to examples in which people are compared to animals. This can be seen in examples such as "Man is like a wolf." There is, I suspect, no animal that has ever been spared from such examples. However, often, these examples do not get to the heart of a consideration or a central idea. Who knows how a wolf or horse really thinks or feels?

### E. The rule-example-rule technique

The rule-example-rule technique (Gage & Berliner, 1996) is also suitable for integrating new content into existing knowledge. The combination of inductive and deductive methods, from examples to concepts, statements, rules, and laws, is a particularly effective link.

This pattern

- begins with the naming of the term/statement/rule,
- followed by examples that illustrate or substantiate the term/statement/rule, and
- concludes with the repetition of the term, rule, or statement.

Example: "In training courses to improve communicative *skills*, these are assigned to superordinate perceptual and *behavioral* dimensions. For example, the communicative skills "content overview" and "state goal and topic" are assigned to the dimension of "clarity in execution." By assigning skills to perceptual and behavioral dimensions, they can be better retained and recalled more quickly in the respective situation."

### F. Use of scenarios/case studies

A scenario or case describes or illustrates a typical situation. Case studies can deal with typical situations or problems in many topics. A good scenario or case study not only sets the mood for the audience but can also be introduced at the beginning or at a new main point. If it is chosen from the experience of the audience, it can also create a link to what the audience is familiar with. It can attract attention at the beginning of a lecture or presentation. It is a good idea to keep returning to the same case or scenario throughout the lecture.

## G. Use of analogies

Hofstadter and Sander (2014) described analogies and concepts as the heart of cognition and thinking. Without concepts, there is no thinking, and without analogies, there are no concepts. According to the authors, analogies inspire thinking and are a resource for human creativity.

An analogy is a comparison between two things that are different but have similarities in certain aspects or characteristics. An analogy can be used to clarify or explain an idea, concept, or object. Parallels are drawn to something that is familiar so that it is better or easier to understand. Analogies are often used in biology and other scientific disciplines. For example, the wings of birds (feathers) and those of bats (flight skin) are analogous.

In a lecture, analogies are used to better illustrate processes that are still unknown to the audience. To this end, the event that is used to illustrate the event to be presented must not only be similar to the new event but must also be familiar to the audience. In this way, an analogy establishes similarities between two different concepts, processes, and objects and stimulates thinking.

## H. Use of comparisons

A comparison is the juxtaposition of two or more facts. These can be topics, objects, or linguistic images. It is important to state the basis for the comparison and the reference points with which the comparison is to be made. Similarities or differences are then explained and discussed.

Example: You want to compare individual travel with group travel. Possible bases for comparison include, for example, social interaction, privacy, or flexibility.

## I. Use of metaphors

A metaphor is a figure of speech that describes a comparison between two things that seem to have nothing to do with each other but share common characteristics or qualities. It is used to make a statement or create a vivid image in the minds of those present by using a word or phrase that describes one thing to refer to something else. The background or the context itself is not explained. Therefore, when using metaphors, care must be taken to ensure that the audience understands the chosen metaphor even without an explanation.

Examples: "The Harbor of Marriage," "The Needle in the Haystack," and "The Wall of Silence."

## 4.3.3 Skills that promote clarity in the execution

Table 10: Skills to promote the absorption of information

| Skills | Useful for |
|---|---|
| Speaking style | Comprehensibility |
| Pace, volume and articulation of speech | Receiving and processing information |
| Unknown terms/duplicates | Fluency |
| Sentence structure | Main signifier |
| Explanatory links | Retention performance |
| Precision | Retention performance |
| Non-verbal structuring | Rough structuring of the contents |

### A. Speaking style

Unclear explanations of an issue make it difficult to process and absorb the information presented (Chilcoat, 1987). A great deal of thought and attention is then required to follow the person presenting and to understand what they are saying. Unclear statements that impair fluency include dysfunctional pauses, that is, pauses that have no function, for example, to attract attention—pauses in which "hmm," „um." or other filler words are frequently used, but also hesitant speech, sentence breaks, syntactically incorrect sentences, or sentences that are difficult to understand.

However, the occasional use of "um" and the like is no indication of poor lecture. It simply cannot always be avoided. Not every sentence has to be delivered perfectly and fluently. Rather, the frequency of unclear statements and sentences determines the impression you give. For example, if you ask a very complex question or if you have to answer a question with a questionnaire, this can lead to stagnation or filler words when formulating your thoughts, but it can also be perceived as very interesting and exciting because a new, unexpected answer is gradually formulated.

Here is a negative example: "We will, uh, today, uh, deal with the topic, uh 'Ontogenesis of communication.' So please don't misunderstand ..., um, I will then present the central points ..., or perhaps in other words, um, the development of communication ..., [then there is a break], um ..., where you have the opportunity to ask ..., or perhaps we do it differently now, that is perhaps more practical, first in groups of 3, then ..., um, the plenary. ... Or maybe groups of 4. Are there any questions about this procedure?"

Here is a positive example: "Today, we are going to look at the topic of the 'ontogenesis of communication.' In other words, it is the process of individual development in connection with communication. First, I will present the important content, then there will be an opportunity to ask questions. Then we will do some group work and discuss the results in plenary."

## B. Pace, volume, and articulation of speech

An appropriate speaking pace and articulation of speech also help to make it easier for the addressee to intake and process information (Chilcoat, 1987). This means that you should not speak too quickly, too slowly, or too quietly. Unclear articulation is indicated by mumbling or swallowing final syllables. Many speakers begin a sentence clearly but then often swallow the ends of sentences and no longer articulate them clearly. However, do not over-accentuate every single word. This also requires increased attention when listening.

To achieve an appropriate speaking pace and volume, it is particularly important to alternate between these forms. Speak important things a little slower and louder; you can also speak unimportant things a little faster and quieter. The decisive factor here is really a change—a variation in the way you speak.

Don't be afraid that your audience will recognize your state of origin. All accents and dialect colorations are refreshing and have their justification. Used in a targeted manner, they can be an effective stylistic device.

## C. Clarify unknown terms/use of duplicates

Feel free to use technical terms whenever necessary. Training and education are not possible without technical terms. However, if (too) many unfamiliar technical terms are used (at the beginning), there is an increased risk that the listeners will have to spend too much time and effort trying to find out what they mean. Such attempts take time and distract from following the train of thought. Therefore, it is best to always explain unfamiliar technical terms as soon as you use them.

Often, however, you are not sure whether a technical term is known. If you are unsure whether the technical term is known, it is effective to use a duplicate. For example, you want to use the technical term "elaboration" and are not sure whether the audience knows this technical term. Then mention the technical term "elaboration" and give the following hint (without interrupting the speech, for example, with a question such as "Who knows the term"?): "Elaboration, the linking of new knowledge with existing knowledge." In this way, you have not interrupted the flow of the speech and can continue. This approach is also suitable when introducing new terms and concepts. Always use duplicates so that the definition or meaning of the term becomes clear and is memorized.

## D. Appropriateness of sentence structure

By sentence structure, we generally understand the order in which words or sentence elements are arranged. As a stylistic device in rhetoric, it is often recommended to formulate short and simple sentences or to use no more than 25 or 30 words in a sentence. However, it is not worth paying attention to this when communicating complex issues and knowledge. It is much more important that you emphasize the important terms and the important parts of the sentence, that is, the main meaning carriers. You can achieve this by linking with speech rate, volume, and pitch (important things are presented a little slower, louder, and with more emphasis). In this way, you ensure that even complex sentences are well processed and understood by the listener.

## E. Explanatory links/explanatory connections

By linking concepts and thoughts with each other, the content to be conveyed can be better understood by the listeners.

Hiller et al. (1969) found the following in their study: "Explaining links" shows that these are positively related to retention performance. These explanatory links include prepositions and conjunctions. Examples are for prepositions: "on, in, at, about, after, as, before, by, but, with, under, over, near, off" and for conjunctions: "and, or, so, since, for, because, as, but, yet, still, while, as soon as, therefore, moreover, in case, though, although, even though." Explanatory connectors are important because they relate facts or objects to each other.

## F. Precision in expression

Avoid imprecise formulations, vague expressions, and lack of precision. According to Smith and Cotten (1980) and Chilcoat (1987), the frequent use of vague and indefinite expressions in particular has a negative correlation with retention performance. As shown in Table 11 the categories and examples have been adapted from provalisresearch.com.

Table 11: Vagueness communication

| Categories | Examples |
| --- | --- |
| Ambiguous designations | All of this, other things, other people, somewhere … |
| Approximation | About as, almost, pretty much |
| Bluffing and recovery | Clearly, as you all know, anyway, of course |
| Admission of error | I made a mistake, I don't know |
| Indefinite amount | A bit, a couple, some, a bunch, a little |

| Categories | Examples |
|---|---|
| Probability and Possibility | Generally, usually, normally, probably |
| Reservations | Apparently, appears, relatively, seems |

*Note:* Categories and examples adapted from provalisresearch.com/products/content-analysis-software/wordstat-dictionary/communication-vagueness-dictionary/, 2024.

The formulations listed in Table 11 cannot be completely avoided nor should they be. Each expression has its own function, depending on the situation. There are situations in which it is better not to be very precise.

For example, the use of imprecise formulations is absolutely necessary in many social situations. It may also be necessary to take a step back and show modesty and/or politeness so that no one is offended by a statement.

For a lecture, however, the frequency of use makes all the difference. When formulations such as "perhaps," "approximately," "somehow," and "sometimes" are used too often, this creates too many imprecise and vague possibilities. The speaker gives the impression that he is not familiar with the topic.

## G. Non-verbal structuring

With non-verbal behavior (voice, facial expressions, gestures, body posture and movement, and movement in space), two possible uses can be distinguished: structuring the content and rough structuring.

Structuring the content: Before the beginning, within the lecture or presentation, and at the end of a section, non-verbal signals can also be used to provide structure. For example, the main points are emphasized and marked by louder, more emphatic, slower speech. Secondary points are indicated by faster and slightly quieter speech. This marking can also be supported by facial expressions (e.g., frowning and raising the eyebrows at significant points) or gestures (e.g., gestures that indicate that this sentence or section is coming to an end, the gestures become less expressive, the arms are still) or body posture (e.g., leaning back when the sentence or section is finished). It is always a good idea to use the possibilities of non-verbal behavior to clarify the speech structure.

Rough structuring: Rough structuring is, for example, marking the beginning and end of a lecture by changing position in the room or sitting down when discussing or answering questions or approaching the listeners (entering the room) before a new topic, a digression, or a loosening-up anecdote. (For more details, see Chapter 7.)

### 4.3.4 Skills for all phases of the lecture

Table 12: Skills for all phases of the lecture

| Skills | Useful for |
| --- | --- |
| Take notes | Memorability and rough structuring |
| Outline the structure | Structure and train of thought |
| Repetitions | Memorability |
| Summaries/Review | Memorability and restructuring |
| Questions | Review, deepening, practicing |
| Visualizations/illustrations | Memorability and structuring |

#### A. Provide opportunities for note-taking/taking notes

Taking handwritten notes or taking notes has the function of structuring and improves memorization and performance (Mueller & Oppenheimer, 2014; Reed et al., 2016).

You can achieve the structuring function by making a short pause at important terms or facts so that the audience can take notes. You can also create a rough structure by pointing out at the beginning that you have planned extra time for special sections so that notes can be taken.

It is good for memorization if you also write important terms on a blackboard/flipchart or present them in the form of a PowerPoint slide. Explain at the beginning that taking notes significantly increases retention and that content can be learned better this way.

It is also possible to write by hand on monitors (e.g., an iPad). There are also apps available that, if necessary, convert handwriting into a text file. However, handwritten notes, in particular, increase retention. While there are caveats to writing, it is also a central and essential skill that offers many benefits to promoting memorization. So, encourage note-taking.

#### B. Outline the structure

Outline aids are hints and structural supports that make the structure, outline, and train of thought of a lecture clear to the audience (Gage & Berliner, 1996). They help to structure sections or organize several topics among each other. Such outline aids can be used in particular if you have not made the structure of the lecture clear right at the beginning through an overview, through the topic, or through the objectives, for example, because you want to create suspense and therefore deliberately only develop the structure step by step during the course of the lecture. Outline aids are also used at the section boundaries and can be combined well with transition signals.

Example: "In the first part of my presentation today, I dealt with the importance of information for the transfer of knowledge, with a focus on the 'I-perspective.' In the second part, I will deal with the importance of information for the transmission of culture, paying particular attention to the 'you perspective.' Both perspectives are important in order to understand and classify the topic of the 'ontogenesis of communication.'"

### C. Use repetitions in a targeted manner

Repeating the main statements in a targeted manner not only serves to identify them as important statements in the sense of an emphasis technique—an indication of importance. Targeted repetitions also serve the purpose of memorability.

### D. Use summary and review

In a summary, the core of the information conveyed, the main train of thought, is presented again in condensed form.

Information is compressed by performing the following:

- Less important and redundant information that facilitated the understanding of the main points (examples, explanations) or was intended to ensure their retention is omitted.
- Details are categorized in higher level, more abstract terms (father, mother, children belong to the generic term family; apples, pears, oranges belong to the generic term fruit) and are therefore omitted.
- The sentences are formulated in such a way that they bring the central statements into context.

A summary therefore represents a targeted selection of the information presented from the point of view of its importance. Therefore, it serves two purposes. First, it serves memorization by repeating the main points to be memorized. Second, it serves to restructure—that is, to repeat or subsequently organize the knowledge imparted. In addition, the intention of the lecture or subject presentation should be made clear again ("The purpose of the lecture was …," "My intention was …").

Three types of summaries can be distinguished:

- Chronological summary (the main points of the lecture are repeated in the order in which they were presented in the lecture)

- Systematic summary (the main points are organized systematically, in contrast to the lecture)
- Summary with a new, surprising conclusion

## E. Review by asking questions

Questions can take on various important functions. These include, for example, reviewing, deepening, practicing, stimulating, and structuring content (Borich, 2015; Chilcoat, 1987). These functions overlap, depending on the time and approach. Make the audience aware of how you deal with questions and for what purpose you use them by presenting the methodological steps (see also "B. Provide a methodological overview" completion).

Examples: "I will give you the opportunity for questions after each section."

"You will have the opportunity to ask questions at the end of the lecture or presentation." "I will ask you questions to remind you of the content of the last lecture." "I will ask you questions to expand on the content of the last lecture."

By asking questions, you can check whether the content you have presented has been understood. If you organize the questions systematically according to the questions for each section, you also create a structuring function. If you ask questions at the beginning of the lecture or presentation, you can specifically practice or deepen the content of the last lecture.

Questions are often used at the beginning of a lecture or presentation to establish contact with the audience. However, this approach is not very successful, especially with an audience you are meeting for the first time. The audience does not know you and does not know how you might react to an answer. Simply present the most important content first and let the audience know when there is an opportunity to ask questions.

Responding to questions during the lecture is not always helpful or necessary if it does not fit into the structure. Signal non-verbally that you have seen the hand signal, perhaps with the verbal indication "I have noticed you, there will be an opportunity to ask questions in a moment," and bring your train of thought or the content to a close. Then, ask the person to ask the question. Another possible response to a question or statement is, "Thank you for the question. I will come back to it later."

Finally, at the end of a lecture or a presentation, after you have reiterated the main points or outline, you can invite the audience to ask questions.

F. Visualizations/illustrations

See Chapter 8 for details.

> ### Exercise
>
> Please assign the following examples to the individual skills mentioned:
>
> "Let me summarize the previous section again: In that section I had assumed …"
> Skill:
>
> After a lecture on non-verbal behavior:
> "Which channels of non-verbal behavior can be distinguished?"
> Skill:
>
> "I will first look at research findings from basic research, then applied research, and finally practical research."
> Skill:
>
> A speaker recorded the exact structure of his speech on a PowerPoint presentation. Whenever he comes to a new section, he marks the point he is at in the presentation.
> Skill:
>
> At the end of the lecture:
> "The starting point of my explanations was K., then I came to the points L and M, then N and finally …"
> Skill:
> "Studying literature does not lead to being able to write poetry any more than studying literature leads to being able to give speeches."
> Skill:
>
> "Elaboration is an important technique for promoting memory performance. Elaboration leads to …"
> Skill:

# EFFECTIVE LECTURING

## Exercise

Please assign the following examples to the individual skills mentioned:

"It helps the listener a lot if the verbal message is also clarified by non-verbal behavior. For example, gestures can be used to illustrate real processes (the speaker demonstrates it: There we went up the spiral staircase, there we jumped over the wall.) as well as movements of thought (on one side, on the other)."
Skill:

"Now pay particular attention to the following: …"
Skill:

"The doctor hates the lawyer because he had sued him for malpractice. Not only did he serve a sentence for this, but his reputation as a doctor was also ruined as a result." (Instead of: "The doctor hated the lawyer.")
Skill:

"Well, somewhere in the warehouse, relatively far back, there is a kind of drawer, relatively large, with and in an indeterminate color, I think greenish, no, maybe yellowish, and there you will find the forms we need."
Please clarify the statement:

"Do you have any questions about the development of this train of thought?"
Skill:

"Management by objectives, the MbO management concept, is based on theoretical considerations … MbO, management by objectives, is therefore a concept in which superior and subordinate managers jointly set objectives and define their respective areas of responsibility for certain results."
Skill:

## Exercise

Please assign the following examples to the individual skills mentioned:

"Giving a presentation requires a lot of improvisation, flexibility, and creativity—characteristics that can be attributed to art. Nevertheless, lectures can also be improved with findings from research, as they also give a rational approach a greater influence. In the following, I would therefore like to talk about how findings from research can be used for the dissemination and delivery of presentations."
Skill:

"He carried off the laurel."
Skill:

"I think I mean ... well, let me put it this way: if it is, uhh, right ... that the state's debt continues to rise, so to speak, then I think, ahhmm, then there is, or let me better put it this way ..."
Skill:

"The following is about creating a positive and good atmosphere with the listeners."
Skill:

"In this lecture, I presented two different, important management concepts: One is the concept of "Management by Objectives" by Peter F. Drucker and the other is the concept of "Situational Theory" by Hersey & Blanchard. The second concept relates the respective management style to the maturity level of the employees."
Skill:

# CHAPTER 5

# Behavioral dimension: Motivation and interest

## 5.1 Sub-dimensions: Individual interest and situational interest

An interesting, enthusiastic, dynamic, and expressive presentation motivates the listener to enjoy listening and promotes retention.

The research literature on interest (Hidi, 2001) distinguishes between two main categories: individual interest and situational interest. Individual interest develops slowly, lasts a long time, and is also associated with an increase in knowledge and values during this process (Renninger, 1990; Renninger & Hidi, 2011); it is rooted in the individual himself. Situational interest is aroused by the environment or by the situation in which we find ourselves; it has to be generated again and again, as many situations are not necessarily always interesting in themselves. Situational interest does not always have to be associated with positive emotions. For example, animals such as snakes can arouse situational interest, but this can be accompanied by negative feelings, such as fear or anxiety. Both categories overlap. Both forms of interest are associated with increased attention and increased cognitive functions and have an affective variable (Hidi, 1990). They also interact with each other. Interest is therefore the result of an interaction between stimulus and person.

The question again arises as to how these forms of interest can be used when giving lectures, presentations, and instructions and how we can motivate our audience. The two sub-dimensions *"individual interest"* and *"situational interest"* of the *behavioral dimension "motivation and interest"* and their associated *skills* are presented below.

## 5.2 Skills for the individual interest sub-dimension

We can use individual interest—that is, intrinsically present interest—for a lecture, presentation, or instruction, for example, in the following form:

Table 13: Skills for individual interest

| Skills | Useful for |
| --- | --- |
| Refer to talents and individual interests | Arouse individual interest |
| Referring to fears | Reduction of anxiety |
| Refer to the motivation to participate | Improving academic performance |
| Demonstrate the relevance of the presentation content | Increase understanding |
| Promoting inner motivation | Autonomy support and structure |
| Interacting with individuals | Intensive interaction |
| Creating "aha" experiences | Attitude toward the topic |

### 5.2.1 Refer to talents and individual interests

Refer to talents, attitudes, or upbringing. Example: Since it can be assumed that an application for a university place or apprenticeship is based on individual interests, this aspect can also be used in a lecture or presentation on this subject.

### 5.2.2 Referring to fears

This can, for example, consist of specifically addressing the fear of failing an exam. However, fear does not have a high motivational effect. On the contrary, in online lectures, the attention and retention performance of students could be increased if those present had to write a memory test again and again. Apparently, more frequent testing leads to a decrease in anxiety about the final test and, thus, to better performance (Szpunar et al., 2013). It is therefore advisable to reduce anxiety through more frequent short tests.

## 5.2.3 Refer to the motivation to participate

When someone takes part in a course or further education, he or she is motivated to learn in very different ways, especially regarding acquiring knowledge and academic achievement.

One student may be interested in participating in class or discussions, while another may prefer to study alone or in a quiet place, such as a library. Still, others may be more enthusiastic about social work, extracurricular activities, or sports.

Interest is considered to be a crucial concept in explaining intrinsic motivation (Schiefele et al., 1993). However, students are often confronted with a lack of motivation, which is associated with a large number of dropouts.

Refer to the motives for taking part in a course or lecture. Ask yourself, for example, "Why are the listeners there? What might have motivated them to attend this course? What motivation increases their knowledge acquisition?"

## 5.2.4 Demonstrate the relevance of the lecture content

One of the motives for attending a course or lecture is that the content is relevant to training or further education. In other words, what significance does the content have, for example, for training or later professional life?

Example: So-called "basic lectures," or basic, recurring information, are also highly relevant. This is because, without the basics, the content taught later cannot be understood or applied; without the basic information, for example, in the area of occupational safety, non-compliance can lead to accidents. However, these connections must be made clear again and again. Only what is considered relevant motivates.

## 5.2.5 Promoting inner motivation

Jang et al. (2010) drew attention to two other important aspects that promote commitment: autonomy support and structure. The results of their study showed that autonomy support and structure correlated positively with each other and that autonomy support and structure increased the predicted students' behavioral engagement, and autonomic support was a clear predictor of students' self-reported engagement.

Supportive teaching behavior is demonstrated by teachers encouraging personal autonomy, taking the student's perspective, providing appropriate challenges, setting meaningful learning goals, and suggesting and offering relevant and interesting activities. It is about teachers encouraging the inner motivational process, using non-controlling language, and acknowledging students' perspectives and feelings.

Opportunities are created for students to take the initiative in their learning. The lecture is geared toward the interests, preferences, and personal goals of the students. (Of course, interest in new topics must first be developed and encouraged. To cater only to personal interests would otherwise prevent the introduction of new and important topics.) A non-controlling language is characterized by the fact that it gives reasons for the task set. In addition, evaluative or controlling information and messages are avoided.

### 5.2.6 Interacting with individuals

Interaction with individuals is only partially possible in lectures. In contrast, short, intensive opportunities for interaction can be created, for example, through small-group work. In a lecture, for example, it is possible to get to know each other at the beginning or when arranging such working groups.

### 5.2.7 Creating "aha" experiences

An "aha" experience is described as a situation in which you suddenly come to a solution through insight and in which this insight relates to knowledge-based interest. In other words, you suddenly gain unexpected insights into a problem that you were stuck on. Aha experiences arouse interest and have a positive effect on your attitude toward the topic. They can be generated, for example, by formulating interesting and challenging problems (Dohn et al., 2009).

## 5.3 Skills for situational interest sub-dimension

As many situations are not interesting on their own and the indications of possible individual interests can (quickly) wear off, it is helpful to also create significant, situation-specific, aesthetic, and cultural events (formal events) in the situation to arouse motivation and interest. This is done, for example, with the help of

- good preparation,
- the use of technical systems,
- verbal liveliness when presenting, and
- non-verbal liveliness when performing.

## 5.3.1 Creating meaningful events through good preparation

Table 14: Skills to create purposeful meaningful events

| Skills | Useful for |
| --- | --- |
| Have a good structure | Cognitive and social development |
| Use classroom management | Organization and planning |
| Increase interaction | Better participation |

### A. Have a good structure

The positive aspects of a good lecture or event structure alone improve engagement and performance and promote the cognitive and social development of students (Jang et al., 2010).

From a motivational perspective, structure gives students a sense of control over the situation and the results of an event or lesson. You are not helplessly at the mercy of the situation but have the feeling that you can cope with the situation and thus develop self-efficacy.

This not only refers to verbal statements but also includes clear communication of expectations for an event, clear guidance of activities, and, if necessary, limits to activities. All of this leads to a motivating learning situation.

### B. Use classroom management

A central aspect of a course is the quality, planning, and management of the information provided; this can also help to increase motivation. These aspects are particularly important in courses or semester events that are held over longer periods of time. In the USA, these aspects are referred to as "classroom management." Important authors on this topic include Theo Wubbels et al. (2006) and Lewis (2008). They have all published fundamental research articles on this topic.

A fundamental idea here is as follows:

- Teachers communicate their instructions and expectations in a clear and structured manner.
- Different activities in the course are formulated in a clear and structured way.
- Step-by-step instructions and procedures are used.
- The planning of activities is clearly formulated.
- The transitions between the individual activities are clear and comprehensible.

Transitions, therefore, not only play an important role during the lecture, for example, as an indication of a new topic, but they are also important for the overall flow of an event. Good organization, planning, and good management of the situation also give the audience a sense of control over what is to come and what is to be achieved. This again generates motivation in those present, which contributes to the management of a situation, including the corresponding positive results. Lewis (2023) and Fogelgarn et al. (2021) described other classroom management skills that are important for a smooth and effective event.

Table 15: Classroom management skills (Lewis, 2023).

| Skills | Necessary for |
|---|---|
| Provide hint | A smooth process |
| Communicate expectations of appropriate behavior | The development of a working attitude that takes into account the needs and interests of those present and is not based on rules |
| Address recognition of efforts | Creating a sense of responsibility and respect for learning; creating a balance between reward and punishment for all Minimizing rewards when the student becomes more responsible |
| Keep calm | The reaction to misconduct by individuals |
| Explain what is unjust and just | Explaining why misbehavior is unfair to others before pointing out the correct behavior or imposing consequences |
| Emphasize on personal and communal responsibility | Appropriate behavior and learning |
| Build a good relationship | Building a good relationship with all students but particularly with difficult students by acknowledging their skills and/or interests. If possible seeking their assistance |

## C. Increase interaction

Studies of physics lessons at universities in Portugal show that the introduction of conceptual questions and peer instruction also leads to an improvement in motivation and better participation during lessons. A lack of interaction between teachers and learners, on the other hand, leads to a lack of motivation (Oliveira & Oliveira, 2013).

## 5.3.2 Creating meaningful events through technical systems

Technical systems are also an effective way of promoting motivation and interest in the subject. Individual variants are presented below.

Table 16: Technical systems to create targeted, meaningful events

| Technical systems | Useful for |
| --- | --- |
| Lecture recordings | Flexibility |
| Padlets | Linking learning material |
| Deep learning | Change your own behavior |
| Student response system | Immediate feedback |

### A. Lecture recordings

A study by New Zealand university researchers (Nkomo & Daniel, 2021) showed that lecture recordings used as learning resources contributed to improved and supportive learning. The availability of learning resources created more flexibility and was seen as an additional resource, not a substitute. Such recordings can, therefore, support learning and, in this way, make an indirect contribution to motivation.

### B. Padlets

Another approach to making lectures more interesting was achieved at Coventry University in the UK with the use of "padlets." A "padlet" is a digital pinboard on which, for example, texts, images, or videos can be stored and linked together. With their help, the students had the opportunity to contribute to discussions online. In a rather small sample of 46 test subjects, 86% rated the use of padlets as more interesting than conventional lectures (Ellis, 2015).

### C. Deep learning

Klein and Celik (2017) are pursuing a technically far-reaching approach with their Wits Intelligent Teaching System (WITS) in South Africa. WITS is designed to provide lecturers with real-time feedback on the state of their students to recognize the extent of their engagement. This engagement is recognized and collected as data based on behaviors and postures that are common in the classroom. These data are used in an observation checklist to create a record of engagement. Common behaviors captured by this system include taking notes, talking to each other, putting one's head on the table, speaking up, and using cell phones.

According to the authors, this deep learning approach should provide satisfactory results for a sophisticated, real-world data set that lecturers can work with to change their own behavior accordingly and, in turn, generate a higher level of engagement. Whether and in what form such systems can be used in US remains to be seen, as they involve a very high degree of monitoring.

### D. Student response systems

Another technical way to make a lecture or course more interesting is to use technical feedback systems, the so-called student response systems. With these devices, students can give numerical answers to questions integrated into a lecture. The answers can then be recorded and evaluated in various ways. This provides students and/or lecturers with immediate feedback.

Hall et al. (2005) at the University of Missouri, USA, for example, showed positive results for this system in a general chemistry lecture that integrated the system. The performance of the test results was also significantly improved compared to the courses that had been conducted without this system in the previous year, and the course was rated as more interesting and motivating.

These results were also confirmed in a study by Cain et al. (2009) at the University of Kentucky with 109 students in a physiological chemistry course. The students stated that the questions used with an audio response system (ARS) helped improve attention and motivation. Through ARS, engagement can be promoted, misunderstandings can be uncovered, and interactions can be initiated (see Gregory, 2013).

However, according to Barnett (2006), it is crucial how the technology is used, and the instructor should ensure that students do not cheat "without restraint" in the clicker tests and that the questions asked are relevant and helpful.

In a meta-study on ARS, Kay and LeSage (2009) showed that the use of this technology leads to an increase in attendance rates, attention levels, participation, and engagement. However, they also pointed out that one challenge for teachers is the amount of time that needs to be taken into account to get to know and set up the technology. Formulating the questions also involves a great deal of effort. The need to respond immediately to student feedback was also seen as difficult. However, as is known in many other studies, students also need to adapt to the new technology and the associated processes. This process must also be taken into account when introducing technology.

A similar option is online student response systems (OSRS; sometimes called SRS or ARS or clickers; there are many different names for this technology). These systems are easier to implement in the classroom because they are web-based and allow students to use any browser and any device to access the responses and "click on." The basic idea is to motivate students, and the system is seen as a supplement to tried and tested methods.

Typically, the teacher creates a multiple-choice question using the software, and the students are then expected to select an answer by pressing the appropriate button on the keypad. While the question (or "survey") is open, the answers are sent wirelessly to a receiver connected to a computer. The software on the computer uses the responses to calculate descriptive statistics, such as percentage distribution, mean, standard deviation, and variance. Once the teacher has closed the question, the results can be automatically projected onto a screen so that the class receives the correct answers along with the associated class statistics. Based on the results of this feedback, the teacher can decide whether to continue with the lesson or lecture, provide further explanation, or whether the students should do an activity to support their learning. This is an original use for OSRS, but there are many others.

### 5.3.3 Creating meaningful events through verbal vividness

We can also create purposeful, meaningful events through verbal liveliness. This involves telling stories, using varied language, and using a variety of examples and metaphors. Easton (2016) showed that narratives can be a useful tool for learning in medicine. Narratives can support several important learning processes, including providing a relevant context for understanding, engaging learners, and promoting recall.

Table 17: Skills to create purposeful, meaningful events through verbal vividness

| Skills | Useful for |
| --- | --- |
| Tell stories about your own subject | New access to content |
| Tell personal stories | Communication of experiences |
| Use case studies | Concepts and problem solutions |
| Historical tales | Linking of topics |
| Use fables and parables | Entertainment and instruction |
| Use examples | Promoting memorability |
| Use analogies | Promoting memorability |
| Humorous remarks | Creating a positive climate |
| Include context personalization | Promoting performance and interest |

### A. Telling stories about your own subject

Stories about your subject can also offer students new access to its content. This is particularly the case if you talk about your own experiences or the experiences of colleagues and relate them to your own subject or discipline. The story can be long or short. For example, challenges in experiments can be presented or an inadvertent misinterpretation of the results, which, in turn, opens up opportunities for new experiments or a new, elegant solution to the problem.

### B. Telling personal stories

With personal stories, for example, you can tell how a particular event contributed to you acquiring a skill or knowledge. You may have experienced and learned about the subject matter, the field, or the expectations of a professional in that field. Personal stories can also be about the time you learned a concept, worked in industry, worked in research, and so on.

### C. Use case studies

Case studies are typically used to present concepts in a situational way. The use of case studies helps attendees apply the knowledge and skills associated with concepts to solve a problem or to understand the significance of the situational use of a concept. For example, the story about Pavlov's dogs discovering Pavlovian conditioning could be a starting point for discussing animal or research ethics or learning about classical conditioning as a concept.

### D. Historical tales

Historical narratives provide information about a topic during a specific moment or a brief development in time. They are therefore well suited, for example, to arouse and link the interests of those present at the beginning of a discussion on certain topics. Example: The presentation of Machiavellianism can be supplemented by a brief historical account of the Renaissance and a reference to subsequent art historical epochs, such as the Baroque and Rococo.

### E. Using fables and parables

Fables and parables are short fictional stories designed to emphasize a particular lesson. In fables, humanized animals and objects are used, while in parables, humans play the main role. Example: In the fable "Animal Farm," George Orwell writes of the uprising of the animals against Farmer Jones and the consequences of the revolution. With the help of this fable, he depicts the effects of tyranny.

F. Use examples

Examples have different functions depending on how they are used. Examples can be used, for example, to promote memorability or to illustrate a point. Examples that alienate an object or relate it to general habits of thought are suitable for this.

G. Use analogies

Analogies also have different functions, depending on how they are used and deployed. For example, analogies can also be used to promote memorability or to illustrate a point.

H. Use humorous remarks

Humor can also arouse interest. It can help to create a positive learning environment, prevent boredom, or reduce anxiety in connection with the difficulty of the learning content. It can arouse interest, promote attention, and provide variety. In addition, humor is seen as a means of putting new ideas on the agenda, provoking change, criticism, and getting out of difficult situations (Adelswärd & Öberg, 1998). However, care must always be taken to ensure that the humor is not at the expense of others.

I. Include context personalization

The inclusion of students' extracurricular/university interests in learning tasks has also shown that this has a positive effect on their performance and learning, for example, in mathematics. However, only a few studies have shown effects on *both* interest *and* performance. Nevertheless, it is a good way to incorporate the personal and extracurricular/university interests of those present.

*Attention:* Pay attention to the right time

When using formal events or components, such as stories, illustrative examples, analogies, or humor, the right timing is crucial. At the beginning of the lecture, for example, short stories or an anecdote about the research subject or the researcher will attract the attention of the listeners. As the lecture progresses, further stories and narratives can be useful to attract new attention or to create a transition to the next or perhaps more complex topic. At the end of the lecture or presentation, for example, another story or example can serve as a summary of the previous content. The spontaneous use of stories and humor is always possible and can also reduce anxiety or tension.

*Caution:* Remarks that you yourself (or the environment in which you operate) consider humorous can have the opposite effect on the audience.

Humor is an effective stylistic device in terms of retention and motivation, but it can also be very dangerous.

### 5.3.4 Creating meaningful events through enthusiasm and non-verbal liveliness

We can also create formal events through enthusiasm and non-verbal liveliness.

#### A. Enthusiasm

Another way to create motivation and interest in a cause is to use enthusiasm. Presenting with enthusiasm creates an environment in which listeners are happy to participate, are engaged, and enjoy what they are doing, and their satisfaction increases (Cruickshank et al., 2012).

However, enthusiasm is difficult to describe. Enthusiasm is mainly shown through verbal and non-verbal behavior and is expressed in a variation of voice, body movement and positions, gestures, eye contact, and facial expressions. Enthusiastic speakers move around the room, use functional gestures to emphasize important statements, vary their voice from loud to soft or from fast to slow, emphasize important statements, and pause before important points to increase tension or create attention, maintain eye contact with everyone present, and support the content they are presenting with their facial expressions.

Keller et al. (2016) defined enthusiasm as the simultaneous occurrence of two characteristics: the display of positive affective experiences and non-verbal expressive behavior. Related constructs, such as immediacy, intrinsic value, teacher enjoyment, and teacher passion, are also included, although little research has been conducted to date (Keller et al., 2016).

## B. Non-verbal liveliness

Table 18: Enthusiasm during presentation

| Non-verbal channel | Little enthusiasm, indifferent, unmotivated | High level of enthusiasm, committed |
| --- | --- | --- |
| Voice | Monotonous, monotone, anxious | Changes in speed, volume and pitch, pauses to create tension, brisk tempo and variety in the way of speaking |
| Gestures | Rare use of arms and hands, arms are often crossed, hands frequently touch each other, dysfunctional | Structuring and illustrative, emphasizing important content and points, use of lively gestures, functional |
| Body movement and position | Only in one place, little movement in the room, defensive, withdrawing | Approaching the audience, functional body movement in the room, body movement in the room is used to maintain interest and attention |
| Posture | Stiff, one-sided weight-bearing on one leg, shoulders strongly bent forward | Functional, standing on both legs hip-width apart, knees slightly bent, forward-leaning; body facing the audience |
| Eye contact | Unsteady, anxious, evasive | Functional, direct, attentive, friendly |
| Facial expression | Expressionless, mouth closed, little indication of the content through facial expressions | Expressive, laughter, open, commenting on content through facial expressions |

CHAPTER 6

# Behavioral dimension: Social learning climate and social atmosphere

The third important *behavioral dimension* in teaching and lecturing is the *social learning climate* and *the social* atmosphere.

The social learning climate is influenced by three factors, among others: the role of the institution, the attitude and personality of the individuals, and the role of the lecturer (Borich, 2015). Since there are few ways to directly influence the first two factors, the efforts and effective skills of the teacher are all the more important.

This includes all actions and skills that help create a productive, social, and pleasant learning atmosphere. A complementary relationship must therefore be established with those present (Bateson, 1985; Burgoon & Hale, 1984; Watzlawick et al., 1985). This means that teachers should create a good and social atmosphere, a pleasant and productive environment, a friendly social climate, and a good mood in a lecture situation.

In such a pleasant and productive environment, people enjoy listening, feel comfortable, and are encouraged to participate. Interactions with others are seen as helpful and pleasant; people are not afraid of making mistakes and are not afraid of losing face or being exposed.

Many studies have shown that a good social atmosphere, a good learning climate, a productive environment, and good social interactions in learning situations lead to better performance and higher motivation to achieve (Allodi, 2010; Borich,

2015; Tausch & Tausch, 1998). Brekelmans et al. (2011) also showed that the dimensions of control and affiliation are valid for describing both the perceptions of the teaching staff and those of the participants. There is also a positive correlation between the learning climate and cultural diversity. It is important to value everyone's efforts in terms of their interests, abilities, languages, and dialects (Borich, 2015).

The *main characteristic groups/dimensions* under which the social learning and lecture climate are described in relation to the social atmosphere are the *sub-dimensions of control*, *rules*, and *affiliation* (cf. Klinzing, 1998; Rupp, 1998).

| Social learning climate and social atmosphere | | |
|---|---|---|
| Control | Rules | Affiliation |
| Dominance | Basic rules | Respect |
|  |  | Humor |
| Socially integrative | Flexible rules | Openness |
|  |  | Friendliness |
| Submission |  | Encouragement |

## 6.1 Sub-dimension: Control

Teachers always have a high degree of control in situations in which they are lecturing and meditating. They determine the content, the pauses, and the extent of interaction between them and the audience or those present.

This form of communication and teaching follows socially accepted norms and rules (Argyle, 2017). One person speaks, and the others listen. This is a tacit mutual agreement. It would also be far too costly and time-consuming to develop new rules and forms for every lecture. In addition, control is of great importance for the effective and appropriate management of lessons. However, too much control can also lead to problems. In turn, control in a lecture can be influenced by the sub-dimensions of dominance, socially integrative behavior, and rules.

## 6.1.1 Dominance

Dominance manifests itself, among other things, in directing, instructing, questioning, interpreting, admonishing, interrupting, excluding, staring down, and directing others according to one's own ideas. Other forms of dominance include a one-sided focus on tasks, a lack of support, and a lack of praise.

These contribute to the fact that fewer contributions are made in learning and presentation situations, that independent and creative thinking is made more difficult, that the formation of one's own values is hindered, and that fewer questions are asked. The ability to work in a team is also reduced, interpersonal activities are hindered, and there is less self-determination (Argyle, 2017; Borich, 2015; Tausch & Tausch, 1998).

Such dominant behavior, as described above, is therefore not recommended or desired.

## 6.1.2 Social-integrative lecturing

Table 19: Skills for socially integrative lecturing

| Skills | Useful for |
| --- | --- |
| Greeting | Beginning the lecture or presentation and gaining attention |
| Acknowledgments | Respect |
| Justification of decisions for a situation | Involvement of those present |
| Participation in the decisions | Reduction of control |
| Avoidance of personal or group-related disparagement | Improving mutual understanding |
| Show consideration | Consideration and recognition of the level of education |
| Rejection of opinions | Distinction between person and opinion |
| Enabling and allowing criticism | Reduction of control |
| Cooperative style for formulations | Encouragement to participate |
| Reversibility of language | Working together and cooperation |
| Use of praise | Appreciation in terms of performance |

A socially integrative and reversible communication style (Tausch & Tausch, 1998) can be used for content-related productivity. This applies to all verbal and non-verbal expressions. The socially integrative communication style reduces control over the learner, reduces dominance, and thus makes listening more productive and enjoyable. This, in turn, promotes retention and is therefore recommended. Accordingly, control and dominance must be reduced for learners to create a good and supportive learning environment.

Borich (2015) described behaviors with a low degree of control and a high degree of "cordiality." Such behavior is characterized by the regular use of praise, the use of informal rules and the possibility for learners to establish their own rules and for the teacher to moderate and participate. In addition, answers are not demanded without prompting, and there is a high degree of work orientation.

A reduction in steering/control and thus dominance can be achieved through a socially integrative presentation style. The following measures and skills, for example, are suitable for this:

### A. Greeting

Use a short, friendly greeting to signal the start of the lecture or instruction; this will attract attention and gain the goodwill of those present. A friendly "Nice to see you," "I'm pleased to see you," and "Welcome to our topic xxy" are important, sufficient, and effective greetings. A grumpy, sleepy demeanor combined, for example, with a short note such as "I've already greeted some of you today; let's get started" is not recommended.

### B. Acknowledgments

Thank those present for their attention, listening, or patience. It is often advised not to say thank you. However, this is not recommended. Quite the opposite. Listening is a (non-verbalized) mutual agreement between the presenter and those present and should not be taken for granted. The purpose of this agreement is to ensure that everything runs smoothly. With acknowledgment, you pay respect to such a mutual agreement. You can also use it to conclude a lecture. You can then move on to other activities, such as answering questions.

### C. Justification of decisions for a situation

Justify your decisions with regard to organizational measures and external arrangements, such as breaks, security, time, place, mood, copyright, access control to documents, data protection, and hygiene measures. Involve the attendees/audience in your decision and explain your decisions. This could include, for example, information about the break arrangements or the drinks or food provided. Mention points during the lecture or presentation when an opportunity will be given to ask questions or when/how criticism can be voiced.

### D. Participation in the decisions

Where possible, participation in the procedure can also be suggested, for example: How long should a break last? Is the 60 minutes you suggested sufficient, or does an extension need to be considered?

### E. Avoidance of personal or group-related disparagement

Use inclusive, respectful, and non-stigmatizing language. Ensure that the content of the speech is free from stereotypes or cultural assumptions that can be misunderstood.

### F. Show consideration

Show consideration for the level of training, questions, and wishes of those present. Show respect for the achievements of those present, and apologize for misunderstandings or if you were wrong.

### G. Rejecting opinions

Disagree respectfully if you disagree with other opinions or unclear statements. Not all "confused" opinions have to be accepted. Reject the opinion, not the person.

### H. Enabling and allowing criticism

Provide the space and opportunity for criticism to be possible and expressly desired. However, this does not have to be allowed at all points in the lecture or presentation or instruction. Such opportunities are available, for example, in clear sections of the lecture or after a summary. Constantly interrupting the main ideas does not make sense but leads to an impairment of the structure. Make it clear at the beginning at which points discussion or follow-up questions will be possible.

### I. Cooperative style for formulations

A cooperative style of wording also leads to a reduction in dominance. For example, not: "I'll show you how to do it now!" or "I will make sure that we find a solution," but: "We will try to solve and answer these difficult questions together."

### J. Reversibility of language

Reversibility of language refers to reversibility of language in the formulations. Use statements to signal that the way you talk to those present can also be used to talk to you.

## K. Use of praise

The regular use of praise has a positive impact on learning and retention. Effective praise is specific and variable, contains information for the learner, shows appreciation for task-related behavior, and attributes success to the effort and ability of those involved (Brophy, 1979).

### 6.1.3 Submission

Submission is a form of submissive behavior and is defined here as the opposite of dominance. It is characterized by the fact that no clear goals are formulated, and the teacher withdraws in such a way that it is not clear what is being taught or what their own opinion is. The content is arbitrary, and the results are unclear because there is no desire to distinguish between right and wrong. The behavior is characterized by great insecurity and/or excessive friendliness, which, however, only has the goal of making everything right for everyone. No responsibility is taken for the lecture.

## 6.2 Sub-dimension: Rules

Table 20: Skills for rules

| Skills | Useful for |
| --- | --- |
| Basic communication rules | Productivity, structure, respect |
| Flexible and explicit rules | Productivity, structure, respect |

Communication is not subject to pure chance but is based on rules; there are also rules for the interactions between speakers and listeners. The rules include, on the one hand, generally accepted conduct that is generally not spoken but is expected. On the other hand, the formulation and establishment of rules of procedure or an agenda makes it possible to agree on rules in a lecture.

General rules of interaction have a universal function (Argyle et al., 1981). If everyone presenting or participating in a speech used their own rules, chose them at random, or behaved and interacted spontaneously, effective lecture and mutual understanding would be a challenge; the symmetry and complementarity of communication would be damaged.

Following generally accepted rules of engagement in communicative situations regulates and facilitates interpersonal relationships. It helps to use a common signaling system or language and prevents mutual aggression so that the interaction does not fail, even when there is conflict or mutual dislike. Further, it is conducive to the productivity of communication, expresses respect for the other person, structures the flow of communication, and begins and ends the interaction.

Based on these rule functions, behavior in communicative situations can be regulated, interpreted, evaluated, reflected, corrected, predicted, and explained (Shimanoff, 1980).

The reactions to non-compliance or breaking of rules range widely (Argyle et al., 1981) from humorous to irritating, that is, from humor to anger. "Usual" rule violations and the deliberate breaking of rules are perceived as highly annoying and impertinent. This applies less to "unusual" rule violations.

To prevent rule violations, it may be necessary to state the rules for a course or event clearly and precisely at the beginning. If clear rules are established, it is easy to draw attention to these rules and, in the event of a disruption or undesirable behavior, to continue with the lecture or lesson anyway (Borich, 2015).

### 6.2.1 Basic communication rules

- Only one person speaks
- Interrupting the speaker is not permitted
- The speaker receives full attention

### 6.2.2 Flexible and explicit rules

- Determine the time available.
- Create rules for the order of posts.
- Signal when you wish to speak.
- Propose specific rules for the process, including, for example, breaking regulations or clear instructions on when administrative topics are discussed.
- Allow non-observance of rules when appropriate
  For example, the lecturer or teacher indicates that they are now not following the order of the requests to speak because there is another important contribution to what has just been said.
- Allow rules to be reformulated: For example, the presenter notices that individual participants are taking up a disproportionate amount of speaking time. To reduce the dominance of individuals, the speaking time can then be limited, or the opportunities to speak can be changed.
- Enable lecturers to adhere to the rules: The presenters must ensure that the agreed-upon rules are adhered to so that, for example, a lecture is possible.

- Enable compliance with the rules through arrangement: The presenters should ensure that the external arrangement allows for an undisturbed lecture or presentation. For example, at a public lecture, you can ensure that the front rows are occupied first so that people who are late can take their seats in the back rows without disturbing the lecture or presentation.
- Formulate rules for the use of aids, such as computers or tablets.

### Exercise

Please formulate flexible rules for your course.

## 6.3 Sub-dimension: Affiliation

Table 21: Skills for socially effective interactions

| |
|---|
| Respect through attentive behavior |
| Humor and situational relaxation |
| Openness |
| Friendliness |
| Encouragement |

The characterization and assessment of effective and good speeches is always associated with positive interactions between the speaker and the audience. The construct of affiliation is used to describe this interaction. Studies have shown that affiliation in discussions (Rupp, 1998) has an effective impact on the quality and contributions of the discussion and that the way in which teachers "affiliate"—that is, work together and control processes during teaching—are important factors for the effectiveness of learning (Brekelmans et al., 2011).

Affiliation includes positive and negative affectives in an interaction. Positive affect is shown, for example, through closeness, eye contact, open posture, and the sharing of private topics. Negative affect is shown through lying, deception, and belittling others in favor of one's own advantage (Wiemann & Giles, 1992).

Affiliation corresponds to and is also found in the behavioral categories such as affection, respect, consideration, empathy, and sincerity versus the opposite of these attributes. This is described in detail by Tausch and Tausch (1998) and Rogers (1983) with the dimensions of appreciation (acceptance), empathy, and genuineness (authenticity).

All these studies indicate that a high level of positive affiliation can create a good emotional and social climate for interactions with individuals, a group, or an auditorium and ensure better work productivity and higher cognitive performance. These findings can also be used for lecturing, teaching, and instructing. The following aspects and concrete behaviors help to ensure appropriate and socially effective interaction when lecturing and mediation.

## 6.3.1 Respect through attentive behavior

Table 22: Skills to show respect

| Skills | Useful for |
|---|---|
| Recognizing the abilities of others | Appreciation of skills |
| Greeting | Showing appreciation |
| Farewell | Showing appreciation |
| Non-verbal behavior (eye contact etc.) | Attracting attention |

### A. Recognition of the abilities of others

Attention behavior involves expressing and showing respect and appreciation. This contrasts with disregard, that is, the lack of attention (Tausch & Tausch, 1998).

Respect for other interaction partners is expressed in behavior that regards them as independent and equal persons without prior conditions and admonitions. This refers to both their mental and emotional abilities. Respect is also expressed and shown in relation to the competence and abilities of those present.

I have to recognize the other person and respect their dignity, even if the other person's behavior at the moment of the encounter may not correspond to my ideas and attitudes. My counterpart must be able to "save face" (Goffman, 1971).

A lack of respect and appreciation is expressed in phrases that belittle human dignity, thoughts, feelings, and possibilities of others. Respect and appreciation toward the individual persons present, as well as toward third parties who are not present, help to improve interpersonal relationships.

### B. Greeting and farewell

How can this be shown in concrete terms and translated into action?

This takes the form of verbal and non-verbal messages and information. Respect can be shown, for example, in the form of a greeting or farewell to the audience or to individuals. Example: The sentence "Nice to see you" is a simple verbal message, but it is helpful and effective if accompanied by attentive behavior. The person is accompanied by facial expressions and eye contact, and when the body orientation and posture are directed toward the person or the group.

### C. Non-verbal behavior

These are all behaviors that are shown on a non-verbal level. For many, this may seem too simple or too obvious. However, these moments determine how our counterpart interprets and decodes the situation, and it is your task to code these brief moments and sequences correctly. Greetings and good-byes, therefore, have a different function here than described in the "socially integrative behavior" section.

> **EXERCISE**
>
> Please formulate sentences in literal speech with which you can express respect in a presentation.

### 6.3.2 Humor

Table 23: Skills to show humor

| Skills | Useful for |
| --- | --- |
| Lightening remarks | Attracting attention |
| Humorous comments | Reducing tensions |
| Wordplay | Attracting attention |
| Funny stories | Entertainment |

A difficult or deadlocked situation in an event, course, or seminar that creates tense feelings among those present does not have a positive effect on the absorption and processing of content. In such situations, humor can be very helpful and relax the situation. However, a humorous remark must not be used at the expense of others.

Research shows that humor has positive effects on reducing anxiety (Ventis et al., 2001), apparently increases retention (Gage & Berliner, 1996), improves creativity (Chen et al., 2019; Ziv, 2008), reduces hostile behavior (Nir & Halperin, 2018), and increases helpfulness, establishes a flexible, spontaneous mood, and encourages others to share personal episodes as well (Borich, 2015).

## A. Lightening remarks, humor, puns

Use lightening remarks, jokes, puns, and funny stories, as well as humorous comments, to take advantage of situational humorous opportunities. But be careful: if used incorrectly, humor can create negative tensions and cause more difficulties than you would like. Negative moods create anxiety and impair the absorption and processing of information.

> **EXERCISE**
>
> Please formulate a humorous remark in literal speech.

### 6.3.3 Openness

Table 24: Skills to show openness

| Skills | Useful for |
|---|---|
| Provide information about yourself | Building trust |
| Taking responsibility for your own thoughts and feelings | Reversibility |
| Answer questions honestly | Reliability |

## A. Provide information about yourself

Openness includes various aspects, such as "self-disclosure" (Wiemann, 1977; Wiemann & Bradac, 1989), honesty (DeVito, 1982), and taking responsibility for your own thoughts and feelings. Part of good and effective professional lecture and presentation is that you also provide information about yourself. Providing information about yourself has the function of building a relationship of mutual trust.

However, appropriateness is important here. Too much information, too much intimacy, and too many surprising "revelations" can also pose difficult interaction problems for those present.

## B. Taking responsibility for your own thoughts and feelings

The speaker should also make it clear that the thoughts and feelings expressed are their responsibility and that they are prepared to take responsibility and make this explicitly clear. Lastly, by being open, we create situations in which difficulties or misunderstandings can be eliminated or clarified quickly and immediately.

## C. Answer questions honestly

Honesty refers to a speaker's willingness to respond honestly to the questions or statements of those present. This includes admitting, for example, when you do not know the answer.

> **EXERCISE**
>
> Please formulate sentences in literal speech with which you can express openness in a presentation.

### 6.3.4 Friendliness

Table 25: Skills to show friendliness

| Skills | Useful for |
| --- | --- |
| Friendly welcome | Optimism |
| Friendly choice of words (avoid abusive language) | Reversibility |
| Non-verbal behavior (eye contact, smiling) | Attracting attention |

Friendliness and kindness have many facets, including psychological constructs as diverse as consideration, empathetic understanding, authenticity, and emotionality. For humans, kindness is always associated with something big and universal.

### A. Friendly welcome

A remark from a conversation partner or a third party about our person, "You are a very friendly person" or "You are very friendly to me," makes us see the world in more beautiful, more splendid colors. It makes us more positive; it makes us more optimistic.

Friendliness can manifest itself in various forms of contact or in the maintenance of a lecture situation and/or teaching position. For example, the verbal greeting "I am pleased to see you" is accompanied on a non-verbal level by a friendly look, a winning voice, a smile, and a clear posture. Take the opportunity to be friendly in your choice of words, using expressions that "win" emotionally. Show positive feelings.

## B. Friendly choice of words

The opposite of friendliness, unfriendliness, can be broadly described as a slurred, incomprehensible "hello," a turning away without eye contact. It is a uniform, routine interaction with the audience. It manifests itself in impersonal glances or derogatory remarks. (There are people who have ritualized derogatory remarks as a form of greeting.) This can often be due to stress, unwillingness, ignorance, or carelessness. None of these behaviors is conducive to starting or maintaining a positive and enjoyable lecture or learning atmosphere.

## C. Non-verbal behavior

These are all behaviors that are shown on a non-verbal level. For many, this may seem too simple or too obvious. These are all behaviors that are shown on a non-verbal level. However, these moments determine how our counterpart interprets and decodes the situation and perceives us as friendly. It is your job to use these brief moments to show friendliness.

> **EXERCISE**
>
> Please formulate sentences in literal speech that you can use to express friendliness in a presentation.

### 6.3.5 Encouragement

Table 26: Skills to show encouragement

| Skills | Useful for |
| --- | --- |
| Encouraging language | Cooperation |
| Use of praise | Promotion of learning processes |
| Reference joint cooperation | Commitment |

## A. Encouraging language

Encouraging behavior can also make a very positive contribution to the overall mood in a situation. It has a positive influence on cognitive (mental) processes and on the cooperative behavior of other people. It can reduce hostile behavior, promote mutual helpfulness, and increase the ability to solve problems creatively.

## B. Use of praise

Praise is also a way of expressing encouragement. Praising behavior has an encouraging effect. Meaningful praise that is expressed regularly supports the commitment and learning process of learners (Borich, 2015). The opposite is discouraging behavior. Discouraging behavior promotes a negative mood and creates inner tension and even fear. However, fear is not beneficial in a lecture or teaching situation. Discouraging behavior also has a negative effect on the absorption and processing of information. Discouraging behavior, especially harsh criticism, affects mental and physical performance (Tausch & Tausch, 1998) and thus has a negative impact on performance.

## C. Reference to joint cooperation

How does encouraging behavior manifest itself in a lecture situation? It has been shown that encouraging remarks can contribute to a positive, encouraging mood. Example: "The next topic is about a very difficult technical model, but together, we will work out the essential functions in this model and plan the necessary time until everyone has understood it." Encouraging behavior also has a very positive effect on the current mood. It improves interpersonal relationships, increases motivation, and reduces anxiety and unwillingness to work.

> **EXERCISE**
>
> Please formulate sentences in literal speech that you can use to express friendliness in a presentation.

# CHAPTER 7

# Non-verbal behavior

The main forms of expression of non-verbal behavior in relation to emotions, states of mind, and attitudes can be found in the face (facial expressions), gaze/eye contact, posture, spatial behavior (proxemics), and gestures.

Example: The expression of friendliness and a positive attitude would be shown in facial expressions in an open and genuine smile; eye contact would be frequent, body posture would be leaning forward and directly toward, and proxemics would be shown through greater closeness (Argyle, 2017). Different types of expression are therefore involved in showing friendliness.

## 7.1 Function of non-verbal behavior in lectures

The main functions of non-verbal behavior during a lecture or presentation are to express feelings and attitudes, comment on verbal content, regulate interaction, and manage the group. In addition, there is the clarification of the verbal content (parasemantics) and the speech structure (parasyntactics), as well as vocal expression.

Table 27: Types of expression for non-verbal behavior

| Places of expression | Useful for |
|---|---|
| Facial expression/facial expression | Commentary, illustration |
| Gaze/eye contact | Attracting attention |
| Body posture | Commentary |
| Spatial behavior/proxemics | Interaction regulation |
| Gestures | Illustration, structuring |

These different forms of expression and their essential functions are described in the next sections.

### 7.1.1 Facial expression

Argyle (2017) described the face, alongside the hands, as the most important and expressive area of the body for showing non-verbal signals. The face is able to show emotions in social interactions in a highly differentiated and expressive way. Facial expressions reveal feelings, sensitivities, and interpersonal attitudes. However, we have learned to control the face very well ("because you look at people in the face"), so we can also show feelings and interpersonal attitudes that we are not feeling at the moment.

Emotions are of great importance to our lives, are always there, and are shown. Facial features, as Ekman (2004) summarized in his study of cultures, are universal; in the private sphere, innate facial expressions are shown, and in public, the emotions are defined by cultural rules. We learn these rules, and we show, reinforce, or conceal an emotion according to the rules given by the culture. Symbolic gestures, such as a nod of the head for affirmation and a shake of the head for denial, are also predetermined and learned by the culture. In Bulgaria, for example, the head is shaken to affirm a statement, whereas in Germany, the head is nodded to affirm a statement.

#### A. Function of facial expressions during lectures and presentations

During a lecture or presentation, facial expressions function to express emotions, interpersonal attitudes and relationships, comments (framing of verbal content, and personality characteristics). It can also regulate the interaction and function in group management.

### B. Facial expression and interpersonal attitudes/relationships

The following basic emotions are visible in facial expressions (Ekman, 2004) and can be expressed: surprise, fear/fear, disgust/loathing/contempt, anger/rage, happiness/joy, and sadness. Emotional expressions are also used to express the interpersonal attitudes that convey a message.

For example, the following interpersonal attitudes can be expressed during a lecture: affection and sympathy, enthusiasm, aversion, or antipathy, interest, and enthusiasm or disinterest and indifference for a topic, evaluation, and approval or rejection and rejection, status and superiority, or appeasement and inferiority.

Affective comments and statements by the speaker through emotional signals in relation to the verbal content help to better understand the speaker. Beyond a general basic mood, short, softened expressions of emotion can be used to characterize and express one's own feelings and attitudes with regard to verbal content. These forms of commentary are very effective presentation tools.

## 7.1.2 The gaze/the eye contact

The gaze is a channel of expression that can both receive and send information. The gaze serves to receive information (being interested in other people, being attentive), and it has an expressive function (showing interest and attention). The eyes are used to open up and make initial contact with those present/the other person. If this contact is unspecific, further signals are required, such as a smile, to clarify whether the contact is friendly or even unfriendly.

### A. Interpretations of eye contact

If the eyes are lowered, this can be interpreted as modesty, uncertainty, insincerity, or as processing complex information. Wide-open eyes show openness, astonishment, surprise, or naivety. Fixed, piercing eyes show coldness and threat. Eyes that roll upward indicate that you are tired, you do not agree with the other person's behavior, or you think they are crazy.

### B. Function of facial expressions during lectures and presentations

During a lecture or presentation, the gaze functions in expression of interpersonal attitudes and relationships, interaction regulation and group management, expression of emotions such as happiness or sadness, affective statements and comments, thereby framing the verbal content, expression of personality, and support of the verbal message.

### C. Eye contact and interpersonal attitudes/relationships

Eye gaze and eye contact are effective signals for establishing, breaking off, or modifying interpersonal relationships. They can show favoritism and affection. People who gaze more are seen as friendlier and preferred. People we like more are looked at more than people we don't like. Gaze can also have a threatening function if we use a direct, long gaze, or it can have an appeasing function if we avert our gaze. More eye contact is used when there is strong cooperation.

### D. Frequency of eye contact

If presenters show little eye contact in an interaction, they are judged to be cold, pessimistic, cautious, defensive, immature, evasive, or indifferent. If speakers make frequent eye contact, they are rated as friendly, self-confident, natural, mature, and serious. Speakers who make a lot of eye contact are said to have almost unbelievable qualities: they are seen as convincing, serious, credible, experienced, friendly, and active. This means that you should make frequent eye contact with your audience and show your appreciation. If you are dealing with a larger audience, take turns looking at a different person in your audience. Avoid staring and rolling your eyes upward when commenting on content.

### E. Eye contact and interaction regulation/group management

People use eye contact to signal that the communication channel is open and that they are ready to communicate or that they want to encourage others to direct their attention where they wish. The opposite is also true: if someone does not want to speak, you can signal that the communication channel is not open by avoiding eye contact. This is particularly important at the end of a lecture or presentation when you ask questions and wait for an answer from the respondent. Those who do not know the answer will not make eye contact. Therefore, the gaze serves as a signal for the start of communication or as a turning point in communication.

In terms of group management, the order of speakers can be regulated by looking at them or looking away in conjunction with facial expressions (friendly glances) and body orientation. Communication rules, such as only one or one person speaking at a time, can be controlled by eye contact: After the end of a statement, look at someone else to get further contributions or answers.

## 7.1.3 The posture

Posture supports the expression of emotions through movement. The functions of posture during a lecture or presentation include expression of interpersonal attitude in the form of sympathy or antipathy, expression of emotions to support facial expressions, affective commentary on verbal content, interaction regulation, and group management, as well as support of verbal content and clarification of the speech structure.

### A. Body posture and interpersonal attitudes/relationships

According to Mehrabian (1972), a positive attitude toward interaction partners (objects and situations) is expressed by reducing the distance and improving visual contact between the interaction partners. However, reducing the distance (see also proxemics) is not always possible in some course/lecture rooms due to technical or structural conditions. Nevertheless, all possibilities, even the smallest ones, should be used. Posture (openness), body orientation, and body inclination play a special role here. A relaxed, casual posture is often adopted toward people of lower status, the opposite sex, and people you like, in contrast to people of higher status, where a more tense posture is adopted.

### B. Posture and commenting on the verbal content

The posture supports the affective statement and the comments on the spoken word, which are shown with facial expressions and vocal expressions.

### C. Posture and interaction regulation/group management

In this context, body posture, orientation, and body tilt can also mark the framing and definition of a section of the interaction. Example: Standing when conveying information generates better attention and an overview. In addition, you give a sign of factual, short-term dominance but also express respect for the audience. This factual and short-term dominance is necessary and important. For group management, body orientation should be turned toward the group as a whole, not away from it, so that the group as a whole always remains in view. Through a combination of gaze and spatial behavior (proxemics), you always signal your willingness to communicate with the group.

## 7.1.4 Spatial behavior (proxemics)

Hall (1976, 1990) distinguished four essential distances that are still valid today. These include intimate, personal, social, and public distance. This concept concerns movement within a spatial arrangement.

## A. Intimate distance (15–45 cm)

The head is seen as enlarged, and the features are distorted. The voice is used very quietly. The warmth and smell of another person's breath can also be perceived. In many cultures (e.g., the USA), intimate distance in public spaces is considered very inappropriate. This situation can arise involuntarily in the subway or on the bus, for example. Then, you tend to take "defensive measures." You don't move. If you are touched at all, you try to withdraw. In a crowded elevator, you keep your hands at your sides and stare into space.

## B. Personal distance (45–120 cm)

At this distance, topics of personal interest and commitment are dealt with. The size of the head is perceived normally, as are the details of the facial features. Fine details of the face are recognizable, as are hair, stains, and dirt on clothing. Voice strength is moderate.

## C. Social distance (near phase, 120–220 cm)

At this distance, the head size is perceived as normal. At 120 cm, the head, shoulders, and upper body are seen. At 220 cm, the same view includes the entire figure. The social, close distance can be found in communication in the office or at a party when people stand loosely in a circle and make small talk.

## D. Social distance (wide phase, 220–360 cm)

The desks in the offices are designed in such a way that colleagues are automatically at a distance. The fine details of the face are lost here, but the hair and clothing of the other person are still clearly visible. Furthermore, the entire figure and the room can be captured. It is important to maintain visual contact during conversations. At this distance, for example, averting eye contact can lead to the conversation breaking off or coming to a standstill. The voice is usually automatically used a little louder at this distance.

## E. Public distance (near phase, 360–750 cm)

At this distance, a vigilant person can undertake an evasive or defensive maneuver if threatened. It has also been observed that at this distance, words are chosen carefully, and sentences are carefully constructed. At five meters, the body looks flat and loses its curves. Eye colors are not perceived.

### F. Public distance (wide phase, 750 cm or more)

Actors know that at nine or more meters, the shades of meaning conveyed by the normal voice are lost; this also applies to the details of facial expression and movement. The voice and movement must therefore be exaggerated and extended. The pace of speech slows down, and the words are spoken more clearly.

### G. Function of spatial behavior in lectures

In a lecture or presentation, the functions of spatial behavior include: expression of interpersonal attitudes in the form of approach and partisanship, expression of emotions, affective communication of verbal content, interaction regulation, and group management, as well as clarification of verbal content and speech structure.

### H. Spatial behavior and interpersonal attitudes/relationships

Greater closeness is seen as sympathy and the search for friendly contacts. The closer people get to each other, the more they like each other, and the better they know each other. People keep a greater distance from strangers or people with high status and dominance until they ask to come closer. Even people from the audience who are still talking or who want to talk keep a greater distance at first. The distance between people of the same status is smaller. Important people or those who pay more are placed higher up (e.g., in the stands).

### I. Spatial behavior and interaction regulation/group management

In interaction with gaze, spatial behavior, or proxemics, fulfills the same function as body orientation and body tilt, only to a different extent. Body orientation and inclination are also less pronounced in rooms with close proximity and distance. With large spatial distances, such as in a lecture hall, body orientation is also possible to a greater extent. Lecturers can move toward and away from people, groups, and objects to regulate interaction, initiate communication, or gain attention.

## 7.1.5 Gestures

### A. Origin of gestures

It is assumed that the emergence and origin of language are closely related to gestures (Hewes, 1973). Tomasello (2020) described two types of gestures used by apes: gestures with intention movement and gestures for attention recipients. This is expressed by the fact that a gesturing ape wants its gesture to achieve that the recipient either does something (intention movement) or sees something (attention receiver). Therefore, Tomasello (2020) further concluded that these types of gestures are the evolutionary basis for the gestures and pointing gestures of human infants.

### B. Gestures and cultural differences

Studies have shown cultural differences in the use of gestures. In Italy, for example, many gestures are performed from the shoulder next to the body, with a wide and round radius and very fluently, which appears more lively and expressive, whereas in Germany, gestures tend to be performed from the forearm with a restricted radius, which appears somewhat more angular and less fluent and lively and (yes, also less elegant). There are also differences between China and Germany; for example, certain gestures that are considered inappropriate in Germany are considered polite in China. For example, it is impolite in Germany to hold your hand (gesture) in front of your mouth when laughing (facial expression), whereas in China this is a sign of politeness.

The use of gestural emblems and symbols is also shaped by culture. For example, the ring gesture (thumb and index finger form a ring) signifies "A-ok" or good in the United States. It may stand for "worthless" or "zero" in other cultures.

### C. Function of gestures in lectures

Gestures are also visible and expressive tools in lectures or presentations. Their functions here are illustration and structuring. When illustrating, verbal statements are supplemented, and objects or movements can be shown. For example, you can show a circle when explaining the function of a wheel. If you are talking about snakes, you can simultaneously make a wriggling movement with your hand to emphasize and complement what you are saying. This creates additional attention to what is being said. You can use the structuring function if, for example, you move your hands downward at the end of a sentence to conclude the sentence, wait briefly, and then continue with your gestures and voice.

### D. Gestures and interaction regulation/group management

You can use gestures, for example, to assign the speaker role or to involve individuals or the whole group. You can indicate the order of speakers ("First you, then you and then you!"), ask for attention, or continue speaking ("Let's continue now!").

## E. Gestures and functionality

Important: In addition to the function of the gestures, their use and execution must also be functional. For example, if you show a circle with your hands and arms, this gesture must be performed completely in a flowing movement. The flow of the movement should not be interrupted. A dysfunctional, interrupted movement would be "unconsciously" perceived as dysfunctional by the audience.

A common mistake when using gestures, for example, is that the hands or arms "fall down," that is, are not executed as a functional and flowing movement. This dysfunctional execution of gestures leads to irritation among listeners. Dysfunctional gestures are directionless, scattered, or meaningless. These gestures can refer to themselves or be "substitute actions," for example, in cases of frustration, conflict, or complex tasks. This is expressed, for example, by scratching, touching the body such as the nose or lips, clenching a fist, or tugging at clothing. It also includes mechanically repeated gestures, as opposed to varying and functional gestures.

The expression of emotions can also be expressed in gestures that are not linked to an intention to communicate but are rather concealed. Such forms of gestures then serve to dissipate or increase arousal and are referred to as self-adaptors. This is expressed, for example, by touching the face or parts of the body. For example, fear and/or caution are shown by tense, cramped hands or hands held together tightly, eyebrows being plucked, or fists opening and closing.

Use non-verbal behavior when presenting. Functionality is always the key. Don't be afraid to make mistakes. Use the skills described here and you will be successful.

# CHAPTER 8

# Visualizations

## 8.1 Function of visualizations and illustrations

Visualizations and illustrations can always be used and have the following functions:

Table 28: Functions of visualizations

| Functions of visualizations | Important for |
|---|---|
| Help with retention | Increasing memorability |
| Visualize | Facilitating complexity |
| Organizing and structuring | Clarification of key information |
| Arouse motivation and emotion | Influencing motivation and emotion |
| Influencing decisions | Creating "inner images" |
| Indirect influence | Abstract concepts |
| Representation of concrete reality | Language and symbols |
| Truth function | Indirect visualization |

### 8.1.1 Help with retention

By repeating the knowledge conveyed in the oral presentation with the help of an illustration, a second learning opportunity is opened up. This increases memorability. Visualizations can create additional meaningful links to existing knowledge.

### 8.1.2 Visualize

Illustrations make it easier to understand complex issues that are difficult to understand.

### 8.1.3 Organizing and structuring

Key information and the relationships between key information are clarified by means of illustrations, in particular diagrams, graphs, etc., or by highlighting illustrations (e.g., in the graphic representation of the brain or the lecture structure).

### 8.1.4 Arouse and influence motivation, emotions, attitudes, and interest

With the appropriate design of illustrations as a content-related "event," surprise or through formal means such as size, color, movement, or contrast and the use of peripheral stimuli, for example, decorations such as a rose at the edge of the picture in the presentation of "dry" facts, emotions, motivation, and attitudes are positively and negatively influenced by the information intake, and a perceptual climate is created that shapes the evaluation of the information.

### 8.1.5 Influencing decisions and behavior

Images are more likely to convey an "inner picture," an inner idea, than language, and "inner pictures" can (often) be recalled more quickly than symbolic linguistic ideas. Recall is related to the speed of decision-making. Decisions and behavior are therefore (often) more strongly influenced by images than by language.

### 8.1.6 Indirect influence

Certain abstract statements, such as comfort, freedom, or democracy, can often only be visualized indirectly. This can be done by simplifying and combining images. For example, the concept of freedom was successfully visualized for decades with a cowboy riding in the desert and looking into the evening sun. This advertising was so successful that the brand name and mention of the product could be dispensed with. This successful advertising campaign was only brought to an end by the legal ban on tobacco advertising. However, attempts to create similarly high-quality visualizations for your own presentations are generally unsuccessful.

### 8.1.7 Representation of concrete reality

Visualizations are very helpful in the representation of concrete reality, as both a linguistic and a symbolic one can be used. This allows facts to be processed quickly and effortlessly. However, there is no guarantee that you will be able to remember these facts better.

### 8.1.8 Truth function

Truth functions and/or abstract statements, such as freedom or democracy, can often only be visualized indirectly (see section 8.1.6 "Indirect influence"). For example, freedom has been visualized for many decades with my cowboy riding across the prairie. This advertising was very successful, but in the end, freedom was not found. As a result of social pressure, the advertisement had to be discontinued. Further detailed explanations of the function of illustrations and visualizations can be found in Kroeber-Riel (1996).

## 8.2 Types of diagrams

Table 29: Types of diagrams

| Diagrams | Important for |
|---|---|
| Process (linear or circular) | Representation of processes or procedures |
| Structure | Relationships between levels |
| Ring | Representation of cycles/periods |
| Cluster | Recognize patterns and relationships |
| Rays | Creating relationships |

Diagrams are visual representations of information, data, or processes (see Duarte, 2009). They can be used to show relationships, connections, or hierarchies between different elements and can help to better understand and communicate complex ideas or systems. There are many different types of diagrams, such as flowcharts,

## 88 | EFFECTIVE LECTURING

concept maps, organizational charts, and network diagrams, to name but a few. They can be created using a variety of tools, such as drawing software or specialized diagramming applications. The following list shows only a selection of the most common diagrams.

### 8.2.1 Process (linear or circular)

A process diagram is a graphical representation of a process or workflow. It can be used to document and understand a process and to communicate that process to others. Process diagrams can be created using a variety of tools, such as flowcharts, swim-lane diagrams, and process maps. The specific symbols and notations used in a process diagram depend on the purpose and target audience of the diagram. Process diagrams can be used in a variety of areas, including business, engineering, and healthcare.

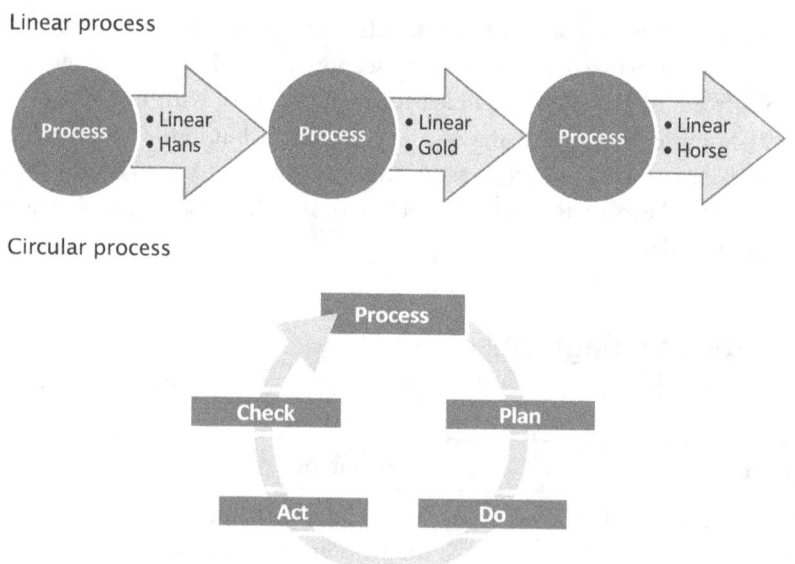

### 8.2.2 Structure (hierarchy)

A hierarchy diagram is a visual representation of a structure or system in which the elements are arranged in a hierarchy, with the most important or general elements at the top and the least important or specific elements at the bottom. It is often used to show the relationships between different levels or categories within a system, for example, the hierarchy of a company, the classification of living things, or the structure of a computer network. Hierarchy diagrams can be created using specialized software or drawn by hand, with boxes or other shapes representing the elements in the hierarchy and lines showing the relationships between them.

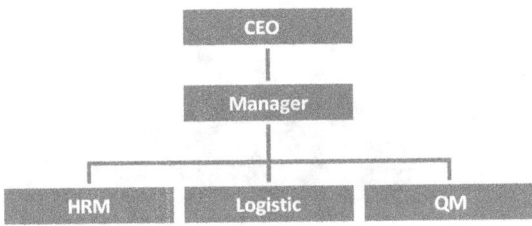

### 8.2.3 Ring

A ring diagram, also known as a polar area diagram or rose diagram, is a graphical representation of data that has a cyclical or periodic character. It consists of a circle divided into a series of equal-sized sectors, where the size of each sector represents the size of a particular data point. The sectors can be arranged either radially or concentrically, depending on the desired visualization. Ring diagrams are often used in various fields, such as business, meteorology, and biology, to visualize data such as sales, solar radiation, or species distribution.

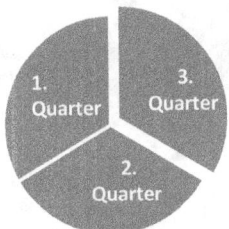

### 8.2.4 Cluster

A cluster diagram is a graphical representation of data organized into clusters or groups. The data points within each cluster are more similar to each other than the data points in other clusters. The clusters are often represented in the form of circles or other shapes, and the data points within each cluster are usually connected by lines or other visual indicators. Cluster diagrams are often used in data visualization and analysis to identify patterns and relationships within the data. They can be helpful in understanding complex datasets and in making informed decisions based on the data.

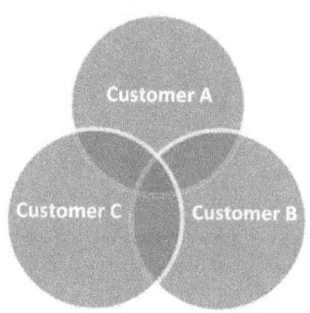

### 8.2.5 Rays

Starting from a point, rays are used to create a relationship. The outer elements are connected to the central point to hold this relationship together and show that this relationship comes from a clear origin.

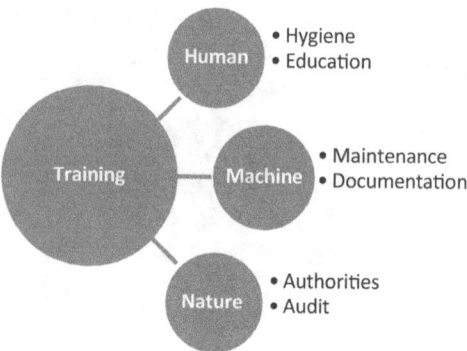

## 8.3 Diagrams as concepts

Diagrams can also be used to represent concepts, for example, a process, a disclosure, a route description, a location, or the effects (cf. Duarte, 2009). This form of diagram can be used to classify, combine, and present complex issues. The following list shows only a selection.

## 8.3.1 Process

A process in a diagram refers to the step-by-step representation of an action or sequence of events depicted in a picture. A process picture usually shows a sequence of events or steps that are required to achieve a specific goal or result.

## 8.3.2 Disclosure

A disclosure in an image refers to the revelation or representation of something that was previously hidden, obscured, or unclear. It can be the unveiling of information, feelings, or even physical objects. In an image, revelation can be achieved, for example, by highlighting details or revealing hidden elements to give the viewer a deeper understanding of what is depicted.

## 8.3.3 Directions

Directions in a picture can be represented by various elements. Here are some examples:

- Arrows or lines can be used to show the path you need to take to reach a particular destination. These can be displayed in different colors or styles to improve readability.
- Labels are used to identify important points or places and to show where you are or where you need to go.
- A perspective can be designed so that you can see the path in front of you.
- Landscape features can serve as orientation points by using prominent features, such as buildings, trees, or mountains, as reference points.

### 8.3.4 Location

A location in a diagram can be represented by various visual elements to give an impression of the surroundings. Here are some examples:

- Landscape features, such as mountains, rivers, or buildings.
- The architecture of buildings or structures can characterize a place and give you an idea of where you are.
- People and activities can indicate the atmosphere of a place.
- Works of art, monuments, or street art can refer to a specific place or region. For example, they can indicate the historical or artistic significance of a place.

### 8.3.5 Influence

The components influence each other. It shows how individual or multiple components influence or interact with each other.

## 8.4 Dealing with data

### 8.4.1 Credibility

Tell the truth. Someone will always ask, and someone will always have good arguments if you don't tell the truth.

### 8.4.2 Meaning

The significance of the data must be clear in the overall context.

### 8.4.3 Getting to the point

What conclusions should be drawn from the data? What results do I want to show?

### 8.4.4 Selection

Select the appropriate diagram for your results. Sometimes, it is best not to choose a diagram at all but just a picture that illustrates the most important point.

## 8.5 Slide design

There are many ways to design slides, and the best layout for your lecture or presentation depends on the content and objectives of your lecture. Here are some tips for an effective slide layout.

| Effective layout | Useful for |
| --- | --- |
| Aim of the lecture | Overall goal |
| Audience | Coordination of content and language |
| Conciseness | Information density |
| Uniformity | Relationship between text and image |
| Arrangement of the elements | Creating meaning |
| Headings | Structure |
| Bullet points | Structure |
| Background | Design means |

| Effective layout | Useful for |
| --- | --- |
| Standard templates | Uniformity |
| Pictures | Context |
| Serifs | Readability |
| Accessibility | Readability |
| Font size | Emphasis |
| Branding | Advertising |
| Copyright | Protection of the author |

### 8.5.1 Aim of the lecture

Make sure that the slides support the overall objective of the lecture or presentation.

### 8.5.2 Audience

Make sure that the content and language are tailored to the audience. Take the audience's background knowledge into account.

### 8.5.3 Conciseness

Make sure that the slides are kept short and concise and that not too much information is shown on each slide.

### 8.5.4 Uniformity of the layout

Use a consistent layout of slides with a clear hierarchy of information and a good balance of text and visuals. Maintain the layout throughout the lecture or presentation. Avoid using too much text or too many small images.

### 8.5.5 Arrangement of the elements

Meaning is created through the arrangement of the elements, which makes the message in a slide clear. This is achieved by (cf. Duarte, 2009):

- *Contrast:* The decisive points are quickly recognized.

- *Arrangement:* We read from left to right and from top to bottom. The arrangement of information and data follows these cultural influences.
- *Structure and hierarchy:* The relationships between the elements are logical and easy to understand.
- *Consistent presentation:* The information displayed should belong together. Grid lines are one tool for this. This makes the slides uniform.
- *White space:* Use white space; leave plenty of space at the edges of your slides and between the elements to draw the eye to the most important content. Reduce the content.

## 8.5.6 Headings

Use clear headings. Use headings to organize your content and make it easy for your audience to understand. Use larger font sizes for headings and smaller font sizes for body text.

## 8.5.7 Bullet points

Bullet points can help break up blocks of text and make it easier to skim the content of a slide.

## 8.5.8 Background

The background is intended as a template for the placement of (image) elements and does not represent independent work. The background competes with the content but is an additional design element. Backgrounds are neutral in color.

## 8.5.9 Standard templates

Ignore standard templates. Try to find timeless visual elements such as line structures, bounding boxes, and color palettes. Look for timeless elements that do not change.

## 8.5.10 Pictures

Images reflect the culture and ethnicity of the audience. They fit the context, represent an industry or a situation, and take into account the present day. Mix and match the images. Create your own image database so you don't have to worry about copyright.

### 8.5.11 Fonts with serifs

Serifs are intended for word sequences that are several lines long. They have small feet that create transitions between the letters so that they appear connected. This helps the eye stay on the line when the text is set close together. Serifs have different weights, so the eye can quickly identify the letter.

Fonts without serifs (sans serif): The shapes of letters without serifs are larger and bolder. Sans serif fonts are usually used in children's books due to their simplicity. As some people find them harder to read, they are often used in short texts, such as headlines, subtitles, and captions. Modern computer fonts are often sans serif fonts.

### 8.5.12 Font families and sizes

Do not use too many font families. For a 2 × 2 m projection surface and a distance of up to 10 m, a font height of 5 mm is sufficient. Headings should be 32 points, and the core ideas should be no smaller than 28 points.

### 8.5.13 Accessibility

Be sure to use clear, legible fonts and high-contrast colors, and remember to add alt text to images so they are accessible to all screen readers.

### 8.5.14 Branding

If you are creating slides for a company or organization, consider whether you need to include branding elements, such as logos, colors, and fonts.

### 8.5.15 Copyright

Do not use any images or texts for which you do not own the copyright. Showing images or texts once during a lecture or presentation does not usually give rise to copyright issues. However, passing on or distributing them must always be clarified in advance. If you take these factors into account, you can create slides that are effective and appealing to your audience.

Visual concepts are mental representations or abstractions of objects, properties, or ideas that can be conveyed through visual media. Some examples of visual concepts are shape, color, size, texture, form, space, movement, or composition. These concepts can be used to convey meaning, feelings, or other information through visual media, such as art, design, photography, film, or other forms of visual communication.

# CHAPTER 9

# Teaching subject content through cooperative learning

Depending on the objective, for example, deepening knowledge, a subject lecture, or a presentation may not be sufficient to achieve this goal. Lectures can therefore be combined with other (teaching) methods, such as group work, discussion, and individual work, to achieve a high degree of interactivity. These methods of cooperative learning serve to deepen the content presented, provide variety, increase knowledge acquisition through social interaction, and improve social skills and mutual cooperation.

## 9.1 Cooperative learning and group performance

Group work, or small-group work, is often described as the ideal, most effective teaching method of all. It is often assumed that the effort required to prepare, implement, and evaluate small-group work is low, that it is sufficient to divide a large group into small groups or have them divided up, give the groups a task, and then simply let the groups work. In addition, many teachers believe that they automatically implement cooperative learning with small-group work, for example, without realizing that they are missing its essential meaning.

The high praise given to small-group work is often based on the assumption that groups achieve more than individuals, whose performance is then (subsequently) combined in individual work (= nominal groups: individuals who work individually and whose performance is then combined). However, research shows that the potential group performance (versus the performance of individual group members combined: nominal groups) depends on the size of the process losses (Schulz-Hardt & Brodbeck, 2014).

### 9.1.1 Process losses

Group productivity depends on the extent to which productivity losses are "under control." Process losses are defined as coordination and motivation losses.

> Group performance = potential productivity - process losses (loss of coordination and motivation)

The question now is how certain structures are related to process losses and what measures are necessary to make small-group work successful.

### 9.1.2 Loss of coordination

Coordination losses are caused by faulty coordination in the work of individual members within the group. Such coordination losses can occur if the group members pursue different goals and/or the work is not divided up sensibly.

Example: In a tug-of-war, individual group members do not pull at exactly the same time and in the same direction.

Groups in which members are in competition or working on tasks that involve competition tend to become unsympathetic and then get in each other's way; less good results are then likely to be achieved.

Example: In larger classes and seminars, individually better grades are achieved for members if the others are worse.

### 9.1.3 Loss of motivation

Loss of motivation refers to a loss of productivity due individual group members (consciously or unconsciously) refusing to participate productively in group work and the achievement of results. The main effect here is the "free-rider effect."

- The "free-rider effect" refers to behavior in which others in the group are left to carry out the work at hand. Group members do not fully contribute to solving the group tasks if they feel superfluous, believe that they cannot make a significant contribution to solving the group task, hold back because others are doing the same, because they do not want to do so, or they have "better" plans. This effect arises in part from previous bad experiences and disappointed expectations. This effect is also encouraged when individual performance is not identifiable or is difficult to identify.

To achieve positive results in the development of the various forms of cooperative learning (forms of group work), an attempt can be made to take measures in six areas to counteract the aforementioned process losses.

## 9.2 Areas for measures to reduce process losses

### 9.2.1 Management and monitoring

Keeping friction and coordination losses in group work (within and between groups) to a minimum requires, among other things, high management and monitoring performance from teaching staff. Poor, stressful organization increases the probability of coordination losses as well as motivation losses. Before starting the group work:

- objectives, standards, rules, and procedures, as well as possible sanctions in the event of rule violations, are explained,
- a performance-oriented distribution of tasks is ensured,
- unrealistic expectations of the group members can be corrected,
- the external environment, the room and the seating arrangement are designed in such a way that disturbances are minimized and monitoring is possible, and
- written materials are sufficiently provided for group work.

During the group work, the teacher should go from group to group, make brief contact with the individuals, and encourage the group, for example:

- help eliminate ambiguities with regard to objectives, procedures, and content,
- answer questions and provide feedback for positive progress.
- help correct unrealistic expectations,
- encourage, confirm, and recognize,
- intervene in the group's decision-making processes in order to reduce unproductive behavior and motivate "free riders" and "social loafers,"

- clarify conflicts between group members, and
- coordinate the timing of the groups, etc.

At the end of the group work, a smooth transition from the group work phase to the tests or the presentation of results should be made possible.

### EXERCISE

What other tasks need to be taken into account during monitoring?

### 9.2.2 Work structure

Work structure refers to the way in which learning is socially organized. A distinction is made between the following:

- Individual/autonomous learning: This refers to learning that is carried out alone and independently of others, directed toward one's own goals, at one's own pace, and in one's own space in order to achieve a specific learning outcome. Johnson and Johnson (1995, 2018) recommended using individual learning as part of a lesson that is fundamentally geared toward cooperation. For example, classroom discussions are more successful if everyone has a comparable level of knowledge.
- Learning in competition with others: Competition is learning in a winner-loser situation. The social situation is organized in such a way that its members have to work against each other in order to achieve a goal that only one or a few people are allowed to achieve. The aim is to find out who is the best or who is the best, to achieve a task faster and more precisely than the others (as in a Formula I race, for example). Only one or a few people receive a reward. The consequence is that learners perform in a way that is beneficial to them alone but detrimental to others.
- Cooperative learning in small-group work: The goals of individual group members can only be achieved to the extent that others also achieve these goals. All group members are therefore responsible for their own success, as well as that of others and the success of the group, and must contribute to it.

The question of work structure focuses on the problem of how much the individuals in the group depend on working together to achieve a goal. The question must therefore be answered as to whether they work better in cooperation with other people, in competition with other people, or better on their own to achieve a positive result for themselves or for others to achieve their goals. In traditional classroom or seminar teaching, each person is basically only working for themselves, their own learning success, or a good grade. Everyone is, therefore, in competition with each other. The lower the performance of others in the course or class, the more recognition is given to oneself. This can often hinder work and lead to "competitive situations." If the intention is to increase cooperation between individuals in the group for small-group work, it is important to reduce competitive situations between group members by creating productive interdependencies.

### 9.2.3 Promoting cooperation by creating productive interdependencies (mutual dependency)

If the aim is to promote cooperation, then productive interdependencies must be established in several areas:

- A. Goal structure
- B. Task structure
- C. Reward structure
- D. Accountability structure to promote cooperation between group members
- E. Competition between small groups is occasionally used to increase cooperation between group members in individual small groups
- F. Control structures/authority structures help promote or hinder cooperation between learners

- A. Goal structure: Although the achievement of goals in individual learning is assessed on the basis of fixed standards (e.g., 85% of the tasks must be solved), performance in competitive learning situations is determined on the basis of the rank that learners occupy in relation to others (the winner, the second best, etc.). Cooperative forms of learning are about learners being able to achieve their goals to the extent that the cooperation partners do the same. To achieve this, the group's goals must be clear.
  Group size: As group size increases, the contribution of individual group members to achieving a common goal becomes more difficult to identify. This also reduces willingness to *cooperate*.
  Group composition: As a reminder, groups can be homogeneous (based on similarity) or heterogeneous. In heterogeneous groups, the small group can only be successful if all group members, including low-performing

ones, are successful. The group goal is only achieved if the higher achievers in the group help the lower achievers.

B. Task structure: Low versus high task interdependence: In some forms of group work (e.g., jigsaw), task interdependence is created to support goal interdependence. For this purpose, tasks/topics are divided into subtasks that are worked on by everyone in the group. These subtasks must then be combined in the group under the group goal to achieve the common goal. Example: Measures are to be developed to prevent process losses: Group member 1 works on "Management and monitoring," Group member 2: "Establishing productive interdependencies," Group member 3: "Responsibility structure," Group member 4: "The control structure."

As each group member initially only has part of the solution to the group task, which then has to be put together in the group for a presentation, for the final test, etc., everyone in the group is heavily dependent on each other if they want to achieve the group's goal and their own success. *Cooperation* between group members is therefore virtually enforced.

C. Reward structure: Low versus high reward interdependence: High reward interdependence is created when everyone in the group is rewarded for the overall performance of the group. For example, each group member receives the grade that the group received. Low reward interdependence means that individuals in the group are recognized or rewarded only for their individual performance—not (or not much) for completing the group task. Traditional teaching in a course or seminar, therefore, has little reward interdependence; everyone works only for themselves and has a good grade. Individuals are therefore in competition with each other, which does little to promote cooperation. The lower the performance of others, the more recognition one receives.

High reward interdependence, that is, that the whole group is rewarded for its performance toward an explicit group goal, considerably promotes cooperation within the group. However, rewarding/evaluating the group's performance alone does not recognize the contribution of the individuals in the group. can no longer be identified; therefore, the contributions cannot be rewarded. This can promote a loss of motivation, such as "free-rider tendencies." A simultaneous and balanced assessment/recognition of individual performance and group performance (possibly based on individual performance and its appropriate balance) makes this problem solvable. An individual's performance can be assessed in comparison with previous performance, that is, based on the rate of improvement.

D. Accountability structure: Low individual versus high individual accountability structure. The measures mentioned under points 1–3 for creating a cooperative productive work structure alone, and even more so in combination, favor individual accountability for group performance and thus also one's own performance. Research shows that when two of the most important elements—a common, explicit, transparent group goal and individual accountability for group success—are present in group work, significantly higher cognitive learning success is achieved compared to "normal teaching." Low individual accountability for group success, loss of commitment to the group, and thus restraint in performance weakens the performance and creativity of the group. The loser is the group and the individual group member: the group performance is weakened, and the individual group member loses enjoyment of the work.

In addition to the measures discussed so far for increasing cooperation in small-group work, attention should also be paid to two other areas: the use of competition between small groups to increase cooperation and the control/authority structure.

E. Competition between small groups to increase cooperation within the small groups: A low level of cooperation among each other is, among other things, a consequence of the exclusive assessment of individual performance. This is because the latter causes learners to compete with each other. However, competitive situations, including competition between individuals in a group, often lead to a stressful social/working climate and to disadvantageous interpersonal relationships that hinder work. However, competition can also promote cooperation between individuals in a group—if it takes place between several groups.

F. Control structure/authority structure: Low versus high participation in decisions regarding the definition of content, organizational, task, and reward structure; behavior of the teacher during mentoring.

An attitude toward learners based on mistrust: "Control is better than trust." The emphasis on hierarchical structures, an authoritarian management style, and group management instruments geared toward external control, numerous rules and regulations, etc. create a working atmosphere that may reduce coordination losses in the short term, but in the longer term significantly promotes loss of motivation and internal resignation. By taking a back seat, you become, to a certain extent, a service provider for the groups, helping to create favorable conditions for the performance and success of the group work and ensuring a good working atmosphere.

The interaction structure in the groups (practicing, discussing, etc.) and the performance of the individuals depend heavily on the measures mentioned.

## 9.3 Buzzgroups

Murmuring groups or buzz groups are a simple but very effective way of deepening and clarifying certain lecture topics with a group size of 2–6 people, increasing motivation, promoting social interaction, and providing variety. This form of group work can be used in a targeted manner and without much preparation. Deepening and clarifying certain content is important if you have the impression that certain important concepts or contexts have not yet been sufficiently understood. The problem or question to be discussed in the group relates to the knowledge previously imparted. Observation gives the teacher insight into what has been understood and what has not. This feedback, which can be obtained by listening or through a short discussion with additional information, is helpful for the entire lecture. Based on this feedback, further points or concepts can be added or repeated. The discussion in the groups deepens knowledge and improves understanding. The immediate opportunity to discuss the knowledge imparted increases the likelihood that the content will be better understood or that open questions will be answered. The use of technical terms and concepts is a good opportunity to try them out for the first time, perhaps in a new context. Studies have shown that this combination of methods uses technical terms and concepts more frequently.

This form of group work also improved the social interaction between the participants. The invitation to form groups that do not know each other (or only very little) leads to the opportunity to make contact and communicate with people they do not know. Many regularly report that this also makes it easier and more pleasant to make contact outside lectures. It can also be observed that this opportunity to communicate very quickly and directly leads to friendships that last beyond the course. The explicit request to always introduce yourself briefly by name to the group first has also proved to be a success. This also leads to easier and better contact, better cooperation, and better interaction later on, which is then also the case in other situations that take place outside the lecture.

By discussing together in a group, participants also learn to express themselves, put their solutions and ideas into words, and can thus improve their communication skills. For many, it can be easier to make a contribution in a small group first than to speak up in a plenary session and present their contribution for discussion. This form of group work also gives the presenter the opportunity to review the previous presentation in the short term and, if necessary, rework it and briefly prepare it for the next section.

Procedure: The following steps are recommended:

1. **Introduction:**
   Bring the topic or a focus in your presentation to a close and announce the formation of small groups (2–6 people). Make the new activity clear through your non-verbal behavior, go toward the group and present the group work procedure and define its rules (strongly defined structure by procedure/presenter—little autonomy for those present). Draw attention to the procedure and the time available.

2. **Group division and instruction of the task:**
   Form groups of 2 to 6 people. It is best to start with a group of 2 and ask each other to introduce. (One possibility is to start with a group of 2 and after about 3–5 minutes call for groups of 4). Name the topic to be discussed or debated, or ask a question that can be answered based on the content you have presented.

3. **Working in mumble groups/buzz groups:**
   The questions are then discussed in the small groups. The small-group works out the result, for example, by the group members explaining the content to each other. As already mentioned, the task is the same for everyone. The individuals are dependent on each other when working on the material; they could also work on it alone (*low task interdependence*); however, the *reward structure* (group performance is rewarded!) enforces a high level of cooperation. It is important to ensure that *each* group member is prepared for the final follow-up questions. Cooperation and a smooth flow of group work are supported by constant *monitoring* by the teacher in order to minimize process losses (*high control structure*). As mentioned above, you also have the option of forming larger groups after, for example, 3, 4, or 5 minutes (depending on the complexity of the question or task). Again, everyone should briefly introduce themselves, share their results, and help each other. Pay attention to time management. Point out that there are only 30 seconds left until the end of the group work, for example.

4. **Evaluation of the learning success:**
   After this short phase in the small groups, one speaker must demonstrate their learning success by presenting the result after being called on by the person responsible (the *competitive* component).

5. **General aspects:**
   This form of group activity must be adapted to the on-site conditions. Not all rooms are suitable for the approach described here. Adapt the approach according to the possibilities. It may be that you can only engage in conversation with those sitting directly next to you. However, even changing the seating arrangements of just a few people can have a very good effect of encouraging social interaction with others. This form of group work can get very loud. Don't be bothered by this unless you are disturbing others in the building.

## 9.4 Problem-oriented, discovery-based learning

Teaching and learning always include the intention that the listeners can better understand the information. Therefore, conveying information merely in the form of lectures or instructions is often insufficient, and further supplementary measures are necessary. To improve understanding and achieve this, the idea is that mediation, teaching, and learning should always be combined with meaningful learning. Learners should, therefore, take on an active role in the sense of constructivism to give meaning to the content. Actively involving learners means developing questions together, explaining scientific phenomena, or solving problems (Woolfolk, 2014). However, a limitation of the constructivist approach arises when there is something to be learned for which basic knowledge is still required. Schön (1987) pointed out the differences between novices and experts in this context. So, the question arises: How can we teach beginners something? As a rule, we provide someone we want to teach something with the necessary resources, for example, chess pieces and a chessboard, and then explain and describe how to use them.

Gage and Berliner (1996) assumed that experts in the field of physics take more time at the beginning of the task but can solve the task more quickly than beginners and work with abstract images of the problem. The experts use a cognitive "schema" to solve a problem (Anderson, 2013), whereas beginners do not have a cognitive schema. Beginners, therefore, need time and space to practice certain skills to a sufficient extent so that a transfer can be successful at some point. Problem-solving strategies can be given by the lecturers, for example, in the form of questions: "How should we proceed with this problem in order to achieve exactly x or y? Which processes have an immediate effect if we change condition A?" Discovery-based learning in project groups or problem-oriented learning are included as methods for achieving these goals.

Problem-based, discovery learning, or project group work (Sharan & Sharan, 1992; Sharan et al., 2013) generally refers to an organization of teaching in which learning takes place through cooperative discovery, collecting facts and organizing these facts and solving problems in small-group work and discussions. Learners should acquire higher-level thinking skills such as analyzing, synthesizing, and evaluating, as well as problem-solving. Furthermore, cooperation and collaboration skills should be developed.

Associated social skills are trained (teamwork and communication skills). At the end of this type of group work, the teacher presents an overview of the group as a whole, from which the group should, in turn, learn. The structure determined by the teacher is relatively small, and the autonomy of the participants, their ability to make decisions, is quite high. The model presented here must be adapted to the local situation in each case. The basic procedure is as follows: introduction to the process, presentation of the framework topic and the problem, allocation of tasks in the groups, work in the groups, and presentation of the results. The following is a detailed description of the procedure.

Procedure

1. **Introduction:**
   The teacher introduces the topic and the group work method. The form, meaning, and purpose of group work (including the development of teamwork and social skills) should be explained. The procedure, organization, rules, and overall topic are determined together with the group.
   a. Finding a topic/finding a framework topic.
      The teacher proposes a framework topic themselves, taking into account the knowledge and experience of the learners; this is usually presented by the teacher, or an overview of a subject area is given. Alternatively, the selection of a subject area (as part of a larger subject area) is discussed together (if knowledge is available), how it is to be researched, and the aims of its research.
      A framework topic results from previous lectures, or the learners develop a framework topic themselves in the form of a discussion.
   b. Discussion of the framework topic.
      Arouse interest in the framework topic and building motivation to work on the topic;
      Reach an agreement on the framework topic;
      Develop focal points of interest within the framework topic.

c. Develop and formulate sub-topics/topics for the small groups.
Once agreement has been reached on the framework topic, the learners themselves formulate various sub-topics that are necessary for working on the framework topic. With the help of the teacher, these subtasks are combined into topic blocks so that they can be used as small-group topics. The support of the teacher is of great importance for the delimitation and feasibility of sub-topics.
d. Discussion and determination of the date by which the overall project should be completed. The teacher determines how many hours, days, or weeks should and can be invested in the project and when the presentation of the results should take place.

2. **Selection of the subject matter to be worked on/division/composition of the project groups and the allocation of tasks in the groups:** The participants each choose a sub-area of the topic and divide themselves into groups accordingly (two to six participants). This helps to make the feasibility of the topics realistic. Care should also be taken to ensure that the groups are heterogeneous in terms of ability, gender, motivation, degree of independence, etc. However, the interest of the individuals in the sub-topic is paramount in this form of group work. After the small groups have come together under a sub-topic, the group works independently to determine the objectives, work steps, tools, and timetable.

The following procedure is recommended:

a. Agreement about the definition of the group goal and the form of reporting: The individual groups then agree on the goal of their work. The goal should be as specific as possible. Only if the goal is described in concrete terms can sub-goals, work steps, and the distribution of individual tasks be carried out successfully. The agreement on the objective of the group work also includes the form in which the contribution developed in the individual group is to be incorporated into the overall project (e.g., PowerPoint presentation, oral presentation with distributed roles, discussion, written material).

Determining the resources: The group should also agree on which sources of information it wants to use. These can be the internet, videos, books, films, pictures, interviews, etc.

b. Distribution of tasks to a group member: The work tasks (sub-aspects of the small-group topic) are developed and formulated in the small groups in the same way that the whole group developed the sub-topics. The subtasks should be clearly defined.

Each group member chooses a sub-aspect and works on it. (It is important that everyone contributes to the performance of the small group and therefore also to the overall project.) Working on the sub-aspects (subtasks) can take different forms: research on the internet, libraries, literature searches, collecting data based on published statistics, interviews, observations, etc. All these forms are (or should be) of equal value. The group (or individuals) may also receive material from the teacher that can be used by everyone in the group.

c. Definition of work steps and intermediate deadlines:
The tasks are divided into work steps by the individuals in the group, processed, brought back to the group, discussed, improved, and coordinated at fixed intermediate dates. For this purpose, the partial results and the documents are exchanged between everyone so that the individual contributions can be put together like a puzzle to form a contribution. Such phases take a lot of time.

d. Preparation of the presentation for the whole group:
This differs from the preparation of the report by the individual groups, as the final phase is intended to create an overall picture from which the entire group can learn (this should be clearly pointed out to the groups). To this end, it is helpful if the individual groups are provided with the topics and objectives of the other groups so that the group contributions can be meaningfully coordinated.

3. **Group work:**
The development of group goals, the distribution of tasks to the individual group members, the definition of work steps, and intermediate deadlines is difficult and requires the support of the teacher through monitoring. This monitoring is therefore of particular importance to ensure that the work is not jeopardized by incorrect planning and unrealistic task assignments (in the case of those who may still be inexperienced in group work activities) or by frictional losses (support means little control by the teacher, with a high degree of decision-making freedom for the individuals in the group). A high degree of task interdependence is required for the quality of the work in this form of group work (often difficult and often only achievable through monitoring, as the groups are allowed/required to determine their own task allocation without already knowing much about the subject area). In the group, the final presentation is also prepared for the whole group (with the help of monitoring).

4. **Presentation of results and evaluation of performance:**
   Once the topic has been developed and the presentation prepared, the presentation is given in a plenary, demonstrating the group's learning success to the others and the teacher. It is difficult to keep to the time available, especially as there should also be enough time for questions, comments, and discussion.
5. **Recognition of achievements:**
   The group presentations are assessed in plenary and by the teacher. The interdependency of rewards is low, as the teacher and the participants assess the work freely. Competition between the groups is not part of this form of group work, and therefore cannot promote cooperation within the groups. The performance of individuals from a group for a presentation is usually difficult to identify. There is, therefore, a risk of loss of motivation among individual students due to low reward interdependence. The degree of individual accountability of individual participants for the group's success is also low, as the contribution of individual group members to the final presentation is difficult to identify and is not assessed.

Such problem-oriented, discovery-based learning in groups gives the participants a high degree of autonomy and requires low-process-loss cooperation within the groups, without which group success cannot be achieved. It should be noted that everyone must be experienced in group work in order for group work to be successful.

Table 30: Degree of interdependencies in the group work characteristics

|  | Goal/task interdependency | Individual accountability | Reward interdependencies | Use of con-competition | Teacher determines structure and control |
|---|---|---|---|---|---|
| Project group work | High | Low | Low | Low | Low |

## 9.5 Jigsaw ("group puzzle")

Jigsaw (Slavin, 1983; 2006), often called a "group puzzle", is a technique of cooperative learning, a form of group work in which individual group members work on *different* subtasks (as opposed to similar tasks), which are then put together in the group.

Procedure

1. **Introduction:**
   The teacher gives an introduction/overview of the material, then presents the group work procedure and defines its rules. (Strongly defined structure by procedure/teacher, little autonomy for individuals in the group).
2. **Groups and assignment of material to be worked on:** The participants in the jigsaw are then divided into heterogeneous *master groups* of 4–5 people (in terms of gender, ethnic origin and ability or selected at random).
   The various subtasks into which the task has already been divided by the teacher (e.g., a biography is divided into "Early years," "School years," "School years," "School years," "School years," "School years," "School years," "School years," "First successes," etc.) are distributed among the group members of the "home group." This can be organized by the group itself according to the interests of the group members. The number of subtasks is equal to the number of members of the home group. Through monitoring, the teacher ensures that there is no friction when assigning the subtasks to be worked on to the individual members of the group.
3. **Development of the material and its didactic design in "expert groups":**
   The group members of the home group then go into "expert groups," in which they then work on their part of the material and prepare it didactically based on the written documents handed out, working together with members of other home groups who have received the same part of the material to work on. During monitoring, the teacher clarifies content-related problems. In particular, he/she helps with the didactic preparation of the material section.
4. **Presentation and development of the material in the home groups:** After the material has been worked out and didactically prepared in the back to their home groups. Each of the group's "experts" then teaches the other home group members there. This must be carried out in such a qualified manner that the group members perform well in the final test (i.e., very high task interdependence and very high individual responsibility of the group members for the test success of the individual group members (Jigsaw I) and the group success, Jigsaw II). The teacher encourages the "experts" to teach effectively (during monitoring).
5. **Evaluation:**
   The type of evaluation of group work distinguishes between two forms of Jigsaw: Jigsaw I and Jigsaw II

Jigsaw I: After all parts of the material have been taught in the group, all groups receive a test that is evaluated individually for the participants and counted toward the grade in the subject.

Jigsaw II: In this variant (Slavin, 1983), group scores are calculated in addition to individual test performance. The contribution that a person makes to the group score is determined by his or her growth and degree of improvement compared to previous performance. More precisely, everyone, whether weak or strong, has a good opportunity to contribute to the group score if—and only if—they do their best. The percentage that a participant contributes to the group score is determined by the number of points that exceed their own average score achieved in previous tests. This is calculated as follows:

a. The base value of each individual is set to five points below the average value of the previous tests (percentage of correct answers).
b. The individual can now earn test points up to a maximum of 10 points by counting each point that exceeds the base value (a). (Students with perfect tests always receive 10 points.)

Therefore, the testing and calculation of individual performance in Jigsaw II is based on the principle of calculating the improvement in individual performance, not on an absolute score or the degree to which learning objectives have been achieved. This is not only fair, as even the weakest student can contribute to the group's success, but it is also particularly motivating. This evaluation system, based on the degree of improvement in one's own performance, is particularly suitable for counteracting the low reputation of students with poor performance and their low acceptance as group members.

Other forms of evaluating the performance achieved can also be used in Jigsaw. For example, the group tournament (as in the teams games tournament [TGT], see below) can be attached to the group work as an evaluation procedure: the instruction of the groups by the "experts." Here, too, performance values are calculated for the individual group members, which are included in the group value.

6. **Recognition of achievements:**

   In Jigsaw I, recognition for achievements is given by announcing the achievements of the most successful individuals; in Jigsaw II, the most successful groups are also recognized in a class newspaper prepared by the teacher. Jigsaw I therefore has a low reward interdependence, as only the individual performance of the group members is taken into account. Jigsaw II, by contrast, has a high reward interdependence, as the group performance is rewarded. (Jigsaws I and II have high task interdependence overall—the group members cannot do well in a final test if they have not been taught well by their experts—that a high reward interdependence is also indirectly generated.)

Table 31: Degree of interdependencies in the group work characteristics

|  | Goal/Task-interdependence | Individual accountability | Reward interdependence | Use of competition | Teacher determines structure and control |
|---|---|---|---|---|---|
| Jigsaw I | High/high | High | Low | Low | High |
| Jigsaw II | High/high | High | High | High | High |

## 9.6 Group tournament: Teams games tournament

The teams games tournament (TGT) is a cooperative learning technique, a group work technique in which everyone in the group works on *similar* tasks. TGT is built around two main components: a *cooperative component* and a *competitive component*.

Procedure

1. **Introduction:**
   The teacher gives an introduction to the material. The teacher then presents the group work procedure and defines its rules (strongly defined structure by procedure/teacher; little autonomy for individuals in the group).
2. **Grouping and assignment of the material to be covered:**
   The teacher then divides the participants in the TGT into heterogeneous groups (in terms of gender, ethnic origin and ability, etc.) of 4 to 5 people. The material is assigned to them in the form of written documents.
3. **Group work:**
   The groups then practice the material on the basis of written documents, which is similar to the material tested in the group tournament. The group works through the material together and practices it by, for example, explaining it and querying each other. As already mentioned, the task is the same for everyone. The individuals in the group are not very dependent on each other when working on the material; they could also work on it alone (low task interdependence); however, the reward structure (group performance is rewarded!) forces a high level of cooperation. It is important to ensure that each group member is prepared for the final group tournament.

Cooperation and a smooth flow of group work are supported by constant monitoring by the teacher to reduce process losses (high control structure by the teacher).

4. **Evaluation of the learning success:**
After this practice phase in the learning groups, the group members have to demonstrate their learning success from the teacher's presentation and the work documents against the other learning groups (the competitive component) (this is usually carried out once a week). For this purpose, three group members from different groups are seated at a table (tournament groups). To ensure that the following group tournament is fair, the three members of the group are at approximately the same level of performance (determined after the last test, class work, or last group tournament).
Here, the three best in the group sit at Table 1, the next three best performers in the group sit at Table 2, and so on. The participants enter the tournament as representatives of their learning group. Every point they win in the group tournament is attributed *to* both *themselves* and their *learning group*. As they play in homogeneous tournament groups against roughly equal strong opponents, each group member has an equal opportunity to contribute to the results of their learning group. (In exceptional cases, when it is not possible to assign the participants to the tournament groups according to performance level, the tournament groups can also be put together at random.) *(High interdependence of rewards, high individual responsibility).*

5. **The group tournament procedure in detail:**
In the tournament groups, the tournament group members alternate between three roles: *Reader, Challenger I,* and *Challenger II.*
   a. The reader takes the first card from a pile of (numbered) index cards (pile of questions), reads out the question, and tries to answer the question himself.
   b. Challenger I then agrees with the answer or tries to challenge the reader by giving a different (correct) answer (if they think the reader's answer is wrong).
   c. Challenger II can also either agree with the answer or, if he believes that the two previous answers are wrong, attempt a correct answer.
   d. Then look in the second pile of cards (answer pile) on the card with the same number as the question card to see whether the answer of the reader, Challenger I, or Challenger II is correct and complete.
   e. Whoever has given the correct answer (reader, Challenger I, or Challenger II) receives a point card. If the challengers have given incorrect answers,

they must return a card they have already won. If the reader has given an incorrect answer, there is no *penalty* (I wonder why?).

> For each question, only one of the three participants is awarded *one* point (if the answer is complete and correct) or *half a* point (if the answer is at least 50% correct and complete) or *no* points. All unanswered questions are considered incorrectly answered questions!

   f. Finally, the cards won are counted up as points and entered on a list. The participants take their cards back to the original working group, where the points scored by the individual group members are then added up (group scoring).

These tournaments are held every week with constantly changing but always homogeneous tournament groups, which are put together according to the individual performance achieved by the participants in the previous tournaments: The winner of a tournament group moves up to the next better table for the next tournament, and the weakest of a tournament group is relegated to the next weaker tournament group. The teacher helps and monitors the proper running of the tournament.

As mentioned above, the reward structure (high reward interdependence, that is, rewarding group performance) and the use of competition (the groups compete with each other) require a high level of cooperation within the group. Individual accountability is also given by the possibility of identifying individual performance for group success (high individual accountability).

6. **Recognition of achievements:**
    Recognition is given by announcing the achievements of the most successful groups and the three most successful group members in a class newspaper (wall newspaper) prepared by the teacher or in a learning management system (LMS) (high reward interdependence due to the possibility of identifying individual performance; in addition, high individual responsibility for group success). As mentioned above, the winner of a tournament group advances to the next better table for the next tournament, while the weakest of a tournament group is relegated to the next weaker tournament group.

Table 32: Degree of interdependencies in the group work characteristics

|  | Goal/task interdependence | Individual accountability | Reward interdependence | Use of competition | Teacher determines structure and control |
|---|---|---|---|---|---|
| Group tournament (TGT) | High/low | High | High | High | High |

### 9.6.1 Group work and online quizzes

Online learning platforms, such as Kahoot, make it possible to create and run interactive quiz games. This is suitable for schools, companies, and other educational institutions to make learning fun and entertaining, and also to organize it in the form of group work.

To create a Kahoot game, for example, log in to the website and create an account. You can then either create your own quiz or choose from a variety of existing quiz templates. You can develop questions with several possible answers and assign points to them.

Once the quiz is created, a game code can be generated and given to the participants. Participants can enter this code on their devices and join the game. The game is then started by the quiz master, and the questions are displayed on a shared screen. Participants select the correct answer from the options provided, and the faster they answer, the more points they receive. After each question, the ranking of the participants is displayed to encourage a competitive spirit. At the end of the game, the winner is crowned. Kahoot offers an interactive and fun way to promote learning and test knowledge in different areas. It is a great way to increase motivation and engagement in the classroom. Groups can also be formed to play against each other. Example of a Kahoot quiz

Questions

- To what extent is body weight influenced by genetics? 70%
- To what extent is eye color influenced by genetics? 95%
- To what extent is height influenced by genetics? 80%
- To what extent is breast cancer influenced by genetics? 10%
- To what extent is schizophrenia influenced by genetics? 50%
- To what extent is autism influenced by genetics? 70%
- To what extent is reading disability influenced by genetics? 60%
- To what extent is school performance influenced by genetics? 60%

- To what extent is spatial perception influenced by genetics? 70%
- To what extent is personality influenced by genetics? 40%

For individual difficult questions, such as schizophrenia, autism, or reading difficulties, information on these terms can be provided during the quiz. In this way, important terms or concepts can be introduced or deepened.

## 9.7 Case method

The case method (variants of which are critical incidents and simulations) is used in medicine, economics, business administration, management, and increasingly in the social sciences, such as education, to train staff in social professions. The starting point for using the case method, critical incidents, or simulations are reliable and valid representations of aspects or elements of real situations. These are usually problem situations that are either predefined or created by the learners themselves (e.g., based on the memory of experienced problem situations). These situation elements or aspects can be presented orally, in writing, with illustrations, drawings, live (e.g., through role-play), or more elaborately, audiovisually with media such as film, video, or computer. Countless such situations have been collected and published.

Critical incidents: If only simple, brief descriptions of problem situations are used as a starting point, then we speak of critical incidents.

Case method: If more complex situations embedded in contexts described in detail are used as a starting point, this is referred to as the case method. The learners react to these described aspects of the problem situations: low-structured responses, for example, in the form of (open) discussions of the presented cases or critical incidents, or higher-structured responses, in the form of verbal, written, or practical (e.g., role-play) reactions. The learners' reactions are based on previously acquired knowledge and principles, and are also evaluated according to these.

Simulations go beyond critical incidents and case studies in that the consequences of the implementation of possible solutions to problems in practical action—that is, the new (problem) situations created by the reactions carried out—presented in the sense of direct feedback must then be reacted to from certain points of view. These reactions create a new situation in which action must be taken.

Critical incidents, case studies, and simulations are aimed at an active, hands-on approach to the situations or cases presented—a problem-solving process in which it is necessary to:

- identify the problem,
- generate hypotheses for its solution,
- decide on the most promising solution or course of action, and
- realize this solution or option.

Therefore, the primary intention of these procedures is to promote the ability to develop (alternative) hypotheses and make decisions for the most promising hypothetical solution. However, the prerequisites for the effectiveness of working with critical incidents, case studies and simulations are background knowledge and skills such as being able to analyze the situations, having a rich repertoire of possible solutions and the ability to implement and evaluate the solutions in a qualified manner. However, these areas of knowledge and skills are also further developed in these processes.

Overall, critical incidents, case studies, and simulations seem to be promising in promoting the skills of hypothesis generation and decision-making, so that these methods can be used to support other teaching methods when necessary and appropriate.

1. **Definition:**
   A case can be used to describe a situation or event in a research document (Merseth, 1996). Cases can be given to groups in narrative, oral, or written form. Other media can also be used: videos, DVDs, movies, computers, multimedia, etc.
2. **Purposes and objectives of using the case method:**
   The following table briefly outlines three possible uses of cases in training, although they overlap considerably. These possible uses are to be understood as priorities in the development of cases and their use.

| Purposes and objectives of use in training | | |
|---|---|---|
| Cases as examples to illustrate principles, theories and models | Cases for practicing analysis, problem-solving and decision-making | Cases as a stimulus, promotion of individual reflection |
| Target: Development of theoretical knowledge by illustrating abstract findings through concretely described events and cases. | Target: Provide an opportunity to practice professional thinking, make decisions, and develop concrete action plans. | Target: Development of personal, professional knowledge based on own experience. |

# TEACHING SUBJECT CONTENT THROUGH COOPERATIVE LEARNING | 121

| Purposes and objectives of use in training | | |
|---|---|---|
| Cases as examples to illustrate principles, theories and models | Cases for practicing analysis, problem-solving and decision-making | Cases as a stimulus, promotion of individual reflection |
| Procedure: Representative cases or cases of best practice are selected that illustrate a particular principle, theory or method. | Procedure: Complex, problematic cases are presented and learned to understand on the basis of scientific findings in discussions. | Procedure: Detailed cases that are astonishing are created or presented and then reflect. |
| Cases are presented, studied in small groups or individual work, then discussed in the course of events. The principles, theories, practices, etc. to be illustrated are applied in advance or afterward. | Cases are studied in individual, partner or small-group work. Written material is made available in which findings are presented that guide and substantiate analysis, interpretation, decision-making, and drafts for concrete actions. | In individual, partner or small-group work, participants study their own cases from their own practice from different perspectives, for example, how certain thoughts and contexts have led to actions and vice versa. |
| Plenary discussion at the end. | Plenary discussion at the end. | Plenary discussion at the end. |

A general procedure for using the case method (Kaiser & Brettschneider, 2015, p. 149) is shown in the translated table below.

| Steps | Goal |
|---|---|
| (1) Confrontation with the case | Dealing with the problem situation |
| (2) Information about the case material provided and independent inference of information | Obtaining and evaluating the information required for decision-making |
| (3) Exploration: Discussion of alternative solutions | Thinking in alternatives |
| (4) Resolution: Making decisions in the group | Comparing and evaluating of the solution variants |
| (5) Disputation: The individual groups defend their decisions | Defending a decision with arguments |
| (6) Collation: Comparison of the group solution with the decision made in reality | Weighing up the interests of the individual solutions. |

3. **Suggestion for practice:**
   a. The case is handed out (written, oral) and analyzed and interpreted in individual work or small-group work (4–5 people); insights, interpretations, opinions, and questions are developed. Objective: Individual understanding of the case (60 minutes).
   b. Large group: Discussion of the case with the help of the teacher, who observes the exchange of opinions, guides, asks questions, and possibly provides additional information. Aim: Deeper understanding, not consensus (60–90 minutes).
   c. Development of solutions, action plans, and actions that can be practiced (30–60 minutes).

## 9.8 Discussion

Discussion, in combination with a lecture or instruction, is an important means of deepening the information presented and increasing the acquisition of the learning material. A discussion is suitable for improving social behavior, acquiring social skills, and experiencing and using social interactions in a positive way. The measures presented here are not to be compared with the formats or "moderations" shown in the media.

Discussion is one of the most difficult methods and is, therefore, often not used at all or only rarely. Many people have had bad experiences with discussions or have never learned how much fun and pleasure it is to use and experience this form of talking together. The behaviors described below are mainly based on the work of Rupp (1998, 2010, 2013).

### 9.8.1 Definition

Discussion refers to a range of interaction patterns, including in teaching contexts. Gall's (1987) definition contains five characteristics that distinguish discussion from other forms of teaching:

A discussion takes place when:

- a group of people
- gather at a certain place and at a certain time to
- communicate with each other interactively,
- using verbal and non-verbal behaviors as well as observation and listening skills to
- achieve teaching objectives.

## 9.8.2  Target areas of discussion as a teaching method

The discussion method (usually supported by other methods such as reading, lectures, or individual work) proves to be effective for:

- mastering learning content, especially when the aim is to retain information over longer periods of time, problem-solving, critical thinking, and higher-level thinking (by contrast, for example, lectures and programed learning are more effective regarding acquiring large amounts of information—again often in combination with other methods).
- changing attitudes: Attitudes (toward objects, situations, and people) have three components: cognitive (thoughts, beliefs), affective (feelings), and psychomotor (social actions). Discussions can help bring about changes in attitudes based on the analysis and evaluation of one's own attitudes and the attitudes of others, that is, to make decisions for actions to prepare. Discussions are particularly suitable here. However, attitudes are difficult to change if the group shares certain (undesirable) attitudes and prejudices with a high degree of conformity from the outset.
- developing moral thinking and judgment: Moral thinking and judgment refers to disputes, problems, and cases with underlying value conflicts that the participants must resolve. It is important to deal with arguments that represent higher levels of moral development than those at which the participants in the discussion are currently at. Discussions are recommended for this purpose.
- developing opportunities to participate in a democratic society (Gage & Berliner, 1996; Gall, 1987): This refers, for example, to the acquisition of social norms of speaking with one another (such as the permissibility of certain criticisms of the contributions of others). Here, of course, the necessary discussion can be learned through much practice—except in systematic training (Gall, 1987; Rupp, 1998)—in other discussions.

It should be pointed out once again that discussions are particularly effective when they are used in combination with other methods. However, discussions are also recommended and effective as a stand-alone method. For teaching purposes, a combination with other methods is often useful, especially when it comes to new knowledge to be learned. For example, it is advisable to give students the opportunity to integrate newly acquired knowledge from lectures into their existing knowledge through discussions in pairs or small groups (during or after lectures).

### 9.8.3 General tasks of the discussion leader

Participants in a discussion have very different ideas about the goals of a discussion, what these goals mean in practice, and which behaviors are appropriate, effective, and conducive to achieving these goals. In contrast to small-group work, at least according to the forms of cooperative learning described above, classroom discussions are very open and not very structured. Thus, a discussion leader or facilitator is useful, if not necessary, in developing and clarifying the discussion objectives and helping the group achieve them.

### 9.8.4 Specific tasks and functions of the discussion leader

The discussion leader has specific tasks and functions. The discussion leader must control and accompany both the content (subject matter) development and the social-emotional development of a group. This is the only way to effectively and sustainably deepen the understanding of the content in a discussion (Rupp, 1998, 2010).

A. Controlling the content of the discussion

Content management includes tasks before the event, at the opening, and during a discussion.

**Tasks of the discussion leader before the event**

| Tasks before the event | Useful for |
| --- | --- |
| Selecting the disscussion objectives | Depending the subject matter<br>Changing attitudes<br>Developing communicative skills |
| Selection of topics | Deepening and supplementing topicality<br>Interest and motivation |
| Establishing a common basis of experience and knowledge | Deepening and supplementation |

(i) *Selecting the discussion objectives. What do I want to achieve?*

- Deepen and supplement the subject matter.
- Change attitudes and develop moral thinking and judgment.
- Develop communicative skills and abilities for discussions.

(ii) *Selection of topics*

- Deepen and supplement the subject matter.
- Change attitudes and develop moral thinking and judgment. For example, current events in which points of view are controversial (e.g., "nuclear energy") can be the subject of discussion.
- Develop moral thinking, for which disputes that are based on conflicts of values should be selected and presented.
- Promote social skills and effective participation in discussions. For example, learning the rules of argumentation or the general observance of rules in a discussion.

(iii) *Establishing a common basis of experience and knowledge for discussing a topic*

This is the case when the discussion is linked to previously acquired teaching material or lecture content. Movies, television programs, and readings are other ways of conveying an understanding of a topic and points of view. However, simply providing information is not enough. Discussions should be preceded by individual work (e.g., reading). It is important that certain points of view or focal points on which the discussion should focus are selected together with the participants or by the discussion leader.

**Tasks of the discussion leader when opening the discussion**

| Skills | Useful for |
| --- | --- |
| Inform/instruct | Same level of knowledge |
|  | Building knowledge for the discussion |
| Formulate goals | Orientation and focus |
| Further, open-ended questions | Stimulating the discussion |

Two tasks have to be fulfilled in the opening of the discussion: the social-emotional preparation and the preparation of the content of the participants in the discussion.

(i) Inform and instruct those involved
- Prepare the participants in the discussion for the content of the discussion (content management). As mentioned above, it is important to bring the participants to a level of information that allows them to participate in the

discussion in a truly informed manner. Only then will discussions be effective. If the topic is new, it must be developed in other forms of teaching (lecture, reading, individual or partner work) before it can be discussed. However, even if a foundation has been laid in terms of content, it is advisable to remind students of this in a brief introduction.

(ii) Make the aims of the discussion clear
- At the beginning or end of the introduction, the aim or possible aims of the discussion should be stated and/or worked out with the participants.

(iii) Formulate an open-ended question
- An initial question (broad or open question) or a provocative statement should then initiate the actual discussion.

**Tasks of the discussion leader during the discussion to control the content**

| Skills | Useful for |
| --- | --- |
| Initiate and stimulate | Maintenance |
| Structure the content | Progress of the discussion |
| Further develop the thoughts | Clarity of thought and contributions |
| Correct the content and form | Clarifying opinions/facts |
| Secure the results | Productivity |

(i) *Initiate and stimulate contributions to the discussion*

If necessary, the discussion leader should stimulate and maintain the discussion, for example, by:

- positive listening behavior (encouraging gaze, body orientation, body inclination, head gestures: nodding and smiling),
- broad and open-ended questions,
- provocative statements, and
- non-verbal encouragement to speak up.

(ii) *Structure the content of the discussion*

For the discussion leader, the aim of structuring the content is to bring the course of the discussion into a substantive order for all participants so that progress can be made in terms of content. It is often sufficient to show the participants the course of the discussion in order to avoid further deviations, digressions, mental leaps, unproductive repetitions, etc. Progress in the content of the discussion should be made visible and encouraged.

To structure the content in advance (pre-structuring), the definition of topics and objectives is sufficient to set a framework for the discussion. Topics or subject areas can also be explicitly included, excluded, or deferred. If there is a fear of the discussion "getting out of hand," the focal points can be specified.

- By structuring the content afterward (restructuring), contributions can be put into an order, or this (possibly implicit) order can be made conscious.

(iii) *Provide assistance in the expression or further development of thoughts*

This support is particularly important in classroom discussions. The discussion leader can do this by:

- Summarizing individual (possibly lengthy) contributions.
- Clarifying/structuring individual contributions. (Paraphrasing, getting to the point: Organize main and secondary points and create links between the points made, if necessary).
- Using exploratory questions/requests (request for clarification, for example, through examples, abstraction, justification) to provide the discussion group with more clarity and comprehensibility of the contribution and thus better intellectual accessibility.

(iv) *Correct the content and form of the contributions*

This means that the discussion leaders must ensure that the participants do not represent or argue for or against something they are not convinced of. This also means not presenting subjective opinions as facts and not distorting the meaning of other people's contributions or facts. The discussion leader should point out the obligation to substantiate assertions, opinions, and theses of arguments if these are not noticed by the participants themselves.

(v) *Secure the results of the discussion*

Discussions remain unsatisfactory if the participants in the discussion do not see a result and cannot "take anything home with them." Therefore, it is important for the discussion leader to ensure that the results are properly secured. This does not mean that a consensus has to be reached; controversy is also a result!

The results can be recorded as:

- a summary provided by the discussion leader, with or without additions by discussion participants,
- a summary by the participants, with or without additions by discussion leader,
- minutes (progress report, results report), or
- distribution of tasks, ensuring task fulfillment and scheduling.

## B. Social-emotional control of the discussion

The discussion leader has three main tasks to fulfill for the social-emotional control of the discussion:

| Skills | Useful for |
| --- | --- |
| Creating a productive social climate for discussion | Productivity, cooperation |
| Creating an appropriate, physically productive environment | Social climate, cooperation |
| Formal structuring of the discussion | Regulation of interactions, group management |

(i) *Creating a productive social climate for discussion*
- Productive listening behavior is expressed, for example, by small encouragements to speak and continue speaking.
- Simple non-verbal acknowledgment ("I heard and understood you"; hm, hm, okay, etc.); praise and recognition, confirmation of the correctness or appropriateness of a contribution; partial reinforcement (recognition of part of a contribution or behavior) (*Important:* praise of the contribution, not the person; praise of a contribution that *really* deserves praise).
- Avoid harsh criticism and discourage rejection. Personal criticism, in particular, is counterproductive and should be avoided.

(ii) *Creating an appropriate, physically productive environment*
- The physical environment, the room, its design, and the seating arrangements in which people communicate with each other have an influence on interaction, the absorption, processing, storage, and evaluation of information and thus on the outcome of interpersonal encounters that should not be underestimated. However, this is not done directly but through feelings.

- Physical environments that are colorful, novel, surprising, crowded with people, and complex generate a higher level of arousal. Untidy, dirty, etc. environments create discomfort and negative moods, which can also be transferred to the perception, processing, and especially the evaluation of information. Interior furnishings can contribute to the feeling of being small or large, oppressed or free, etc.
- A functional room arrangement helps to cope with the complex requirements of dealing with groups of 25 to 30 people, to save teaching time, and to avoid unnecessary interruptions, delays, and idle time, which often lead to disruptions, and thus also to facilitate group management. Based on Evertson and Emmer's (2013) study, five guidelines can be formulated for the arrangement of a teaching setting from the point of view of "facilitating group management":
  - Design the room arrangement so that it is compatible with your teaching objectives and activities (example: subject lecture, individual work, partner work, group work)
  - Ensure that the parties involved can easily view all the locations from which information is provided without having to change the arrangements.
  - Arrange the furniture so that areas of heavy through traffic remain free of congestion and chaos (e.g., exits, lectern) and leave enough space for each individual so that you can monitor group or individual work!
  - Ensure that everyone involved can be easily seen by the teacher from anywhere in the room! (Example: whether someone needs help, whether someone is being disruptive)
  - Ensure that frequently used teaching and learning materials and devices required for work (e.g., computers) are accessible without disruption.

(iii) *Formal structuring of the discussion (regulation of interactions, group management)*

The discussion leader must ensure that everything runs smoothly. This includes (according to Bridges, 1979):

- Maintaining peacefulness and the order of the discussion are maintained. This means that the discussion leader is largely responsible for ensuring that, for example, general rules of conduct are observed, speakers always have the full attention of others, the order of participants in the discussion follows rules, and only one person speaks at a time.

– Guaranteeing respect among the participants, their equality and freedom to express themselves. This includes ensuring that all participants in the discussion have an equal right to contribute to the clarification of the matter. Discussion leaders must, therefore, ensure that contributions (or individuals) are not ignored, monopolized, or ignored.
The discussion should not be interrupted by individual participants, interruptions of speeches, insults, personal insults, etc.

## 9.9 Model of direct instruction

One of the most successful methods of teaching and imparting information when little is known about a subject is the direct instruction model. The model combines instruction with repetition, group work, discussion, and individual learning. Rosenshine and Stephens (1986) investigated the conditions associated with improved performance in the classroom, focusing on direct teaching methods. The authors recommended that the classroom routine for teaching should consist of daily review, presentation of new material, guided practice, correction and feedback, independent practice, and weekly and monthly reviews. Rosenshine and Stevens (1986) pointed out that greater performance gains result from teacher-led instruction when it is systematic and provides feedback. The authors describe the ideal learning environment as one in which, first, the teacher is responsible and, second, clear objectives are set. This means that there is sufficient time for teaching, for observing performance, and for the teacher to question learners' responses. The teacher is characterized by direct professional competence in all of these criteria in order to meet the requirements for direct instruction. The phases of interactive and adaptive content delivery described in Chapter 11 were revised and modified based on Rosenshine and Stevens (1986), Rupp and Klinzing (1999, 2008), and Rupp (2021). For details, see Part II.

# PART II

# TRAINING PROGRAM: INTERACTIVE AND ADAPTIVE TEACHING OF SUBJECT CONTENT

The evaluated microteaching training program "Interactive and adaptive teaching of subject content" with concepts, tasks, and exercises is described below. The training program has been successfully evaluated in teacher training at the secondary level, with results showing significant improvement in skills (Rupp, 2015). The training program can be used individually to systematically improve or expand one's own communicative skills and teaching behaviors.

The elements described in the following table are necessary for a systematic microteaching training program.

Table 33: Elements of a systematic microteaching training program

| Elements of a systematic training program | Important for |
|---|---|
| Conceptual framework | Theoretical foundations and state of research |
| The training concept | Overall concept of the training program in terms of practical exercises with video recordings and feedback |
| Effectiveness and appropriateness of behaviors | Development and expansion of communicative teaching behaviors |
| The dimensions | Definition and selection of categories for the content of the training program |
| The contents of the training program | The content of the training program |
| The evaluation | Review of effectiveness Improvement of the state of research |

CHAPTER 10

# Conceptual framework for interactive and adaptive teaching of subject content

## 10.1 Interactive lecturing

Interactive lecturing is a teaching method in which students are involved in the learning process through activities such as working and solving problems, peer instruction, discussion, or the use of voting systems. The lessons are designed to achieve an increased exchange between teachers and students in relation to the content. These approaches are intended to promote active learning, increase attention and motivation, and improve mutual satisfaction and retention. Biggs (1996) pointed out that it is important to actively engage with learning content to promote learning.

However, in a study on the effectiveness of traditional lectures compared to interactive lectures among engineers in the Netherlands, the results are unclear (van Dijk et al., 2001). The authors showed that in engineering education, learning outcomes do not differ greatly in interactive lectures compared to traditional lectures, as there are indirect ways, such as the use of humor and nonverbal behavior, to influence students. Interactive teaching does not automatically lead to active cognitive experiences for students. A student can also choose not to think about a question. Conversely, a traditional lecture does not automatically lead to passive students who simply accept the information without thinking about it. Nevertheless, an improvement and increase in motivation are achieved through participation in lectures. The results also showed that the students rated the opportunities for interaction and participation as very positive and that they rated their own motivation better. According to the authors, creating a friendly and interactive atmosphere alone is not enough for interactive lectures. Teachers must explain the methods, procedures, and expectations to the students in detail, draw their attention to these aspects, and encourage them to ask questions if they are unable to follow the explanations.

## 10.2 Adaptive teaching

Adaptive teaching adapts different teaching methods or approaches to different target groups with different knowledge, abilities, and skills to enable qualified teaching-learning processes. The theoretical basis for this concept can be found in studies by Randi and Corno (2005) and Corno (2008). This is based on the assumption that the teacher has mastered the subject content being taught and that the content and knowledge being taught are reliable.

Teachers should be able to react to complex challenges during the teaching process while consistently coordinating and taking into account teaching objectives, learning content, teaching methods and teaching strategies, and the results of the diagnosis of the target audience's knowledge and prior experience during preparation. In adaptive teaching, teaching is differentiated according to the audience's abilities and needs. Differences in performance in a group or course in terms of knowledge and skills are always a challenge for all teachers.

In the concept of adaptive teaching, teachers align methods and objectives at the micro level with the knowledge and previous experience of the students or course participants. The idea and expectation that course participants will always adapt to their expected performance also plays a role here. The concept of adaptive teaching distinguishes between the macro and micro levels (Corno, 2008).

### 10.2.1 Macro level

At the macro level, the institution often formulates guidelines, content, and topics for the organization of courses or teaching. These include topics such as digital learning platforms, digitalization of teaching, examination performance, values, and norms. All of these topics are specified at the institutional level and are generally used explicitly for the curriculum, for the selection and composition of content, and for courses and seminars (Cruickshank et al., 2012). Other topics are, for example, heterogeneity/diversity and digitalization. These can be described in detail below.

- Heterogeneity/diversity
  The heterogeneity of the groups includes:
  - *Personality traits and attitudes*: Groups can be made up of members with similar personality traits (e.g., age, gender, extraversion, impulsivity, emotional stability, and intellectual openness), interpersonal orientations (e.g., hostility), and attitudes (e.g., sympathy for certain content, objects, institutions, and situations). Not all of these personality traits and attitudes are apparent at first glance.
  - *Knowledge base*: The individual members of a group have different knowledge bases and different knowledge and prior knowledge. Individual learning requirements can be very heterogeneous.
  - *Intelligence*: The individual members of a group also differ in terms of their intelligence, that is, the speed with which they absorb information, how much information they can store in their memory, and how they can retrieve this information from their working and/or long-term memory.
  - *Motivation*: The individual members of a group are motivated to varying degrees and differ in terms of their willingness to learn, their fears, and their self-efficacy. Self-efficacy is the ability to attribute effectiveness to one's own abilities and find a solution to difficult tasks. If you fail at a task, the reason for the failure is seen in your own performance; you don't see the reason for the failure in others. You try again to solve this task and work out new possibilities.
  - *Metacognition*: The individual members of a group also differ in terms of which strategies and approaches can be used to solve a problem or task, as well as in their ability (see also *motivation*) to critically scrutinize and evaluate their own solutions.
  - *Diversity* as a guiding principle for the composition of a group in education is desirable. Two aspects can be distinguished here. One is the added value of talents, opinions, and views (pluralism), and the other is equal opportunities. The added value of many talents and opinions can enrich a group and make new, previously unknown experiences possible for the individual or the group. Equal opportunities refer to the right to gain access to an educational institution regardless of the individual. Equal opportunity means that everyone is given the opportunity to participate in group work according to their abilities. However, diversity alone cannot improve

a group's performance in certain tasks. The type of task is always decisive for the success of a group (Steiner, 1972). A group can only be as good as its best member. However, if everyone knows equally little or everyone is equally poor in their performance level and motivation, measures must be taken to impart, promote, and deepen the necessary knowledge and skills to enable the group to solve complex tasks and problems.

- Digitalization
  - Digitalization in adaptive teaching refers to the integration of technology and digital tools into the teaching and learning process. This can take many forms, such as the use of online platforms to deliver course content, the use of AI educational software to support learning and assessment, or the use of social media and other online tools to facilitate communication and collaboration between learners and teachers. The aim of digitalization is to improve the efficiency and effectiveness of the individual learning process and to offer new and innovative ways of engaging with the subject matter. The use of a suitable learning platform, conferencing software, or tablets can therefore be easily integrated into the concept of adaptive instruction or teaching. To this end, the external framework conditions and rules, such as when, how, and for which tasks a tablet or access to information on the internet may be used, must be clarified and communicated. The instructor must clarify which learning platform will be used and how the relevant data and information will be made available. There are many opportunities for feedback and checking learning progress via digital concepts. The procedures must be made transparent. But sometimes it can also be best to teach over a longer period of time without any digital aids. Don't be afraid to implement this approach.

## 10.2.2 Micro level

The term micro-adaptation is best defined as continuous assessment and learning about what is being taught and how it is being taught. Micro-adaptations are crucial; they represent direct feedback from the teacher to the person learning, and they are deeply psychological.

Adaptive teaching and learning do not use one approach or one form of teaching for the learners. Adaptive teachers assess, for example, the different abilities of students in a course or seminar. In many studies, the theoretical requirements for adaptive teaching have been described using the terms variation and flexibility (Corno, 2008). These two behavioral dimensions are taken up for this training program, expanded by the dimensions of evaluation and assessment, and the necessary behaviors are assigned and described.

The integration of interactive presentation and adaptive teaching leads to the effective lecturing and teaching of subject-specific content.

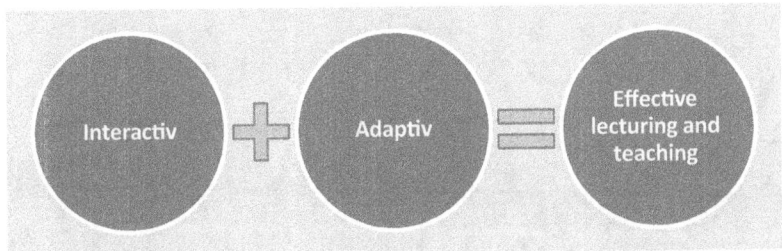

The concept is suitable if you want to promote interactive and adaptive teaching and learning in your course rather than just traditional lecturing. In addition to imparting information, other activities are combined to enable students to take even more responsibility for their own learning. To achieve this, teachers need effective skills. These can be acquired, refined, supplemented, and practiced very well through a systematically structured microteaching training program. All the conceptual components of a microteaching training program are described below. The training program can be used individually to systematically improve or expand one's own skills.

# CHAPTER 11

# The training concept

## 11.1 The microteaching concept

The training program described here uses the very successful concept of microteaching. Microteaching concepts focus on the targeted development and expansion of specific teaching skills through the acquisition of individual behaviors. They are often characterized by the fact that they are geared toward a clear set of target behaviors. These target behaviors are to be newly acquired through repeated practice. However, it is also possible to further develop and improve behaviors that

Table 34: Microteaching training concept

| Microteaching concept and training components | Important for |
|---|---|
| Use background knowledge | Reference framework for objectives, content and planning |
| Conceptual structures for the analysis | Organize and analyze communicative situations |
| Generate hypotheses and decisions | Reducing the complexity of actions |
| Perform actions | Controlled practicing with video recordings |
| Reflection | Reflect on the effects of actions |

are already in the repertoire. These behaviors are specifically described and practiced in specially designed, simplified, and controlled laboratory situations. The advantage of these laboratory situations over normal situations is that they are relatively safe, risk-free, economically produced practice opportunities with a reduced degree of complexity. These five- to ten-minute exercises take place in small groups of four to six students or teachers, in which previously developed teaching strategies, learning skills, target behaviors, or practices can be learned through repeated practice. This process includes intensive feedback (video recordings, observation procedures, and feedback from a supervisor and/or the group). These procedures were developed at Stanford University by Allen and Ryan (1969) and include a series of teaching skills that are considered fundamental. Written material for the acquisition of these behaviors was created with theoretical and practical information and model films. The individual teaching skills were trained in several practice sequences consisting of first attempt—feedback using video recordings, feedback (supervisor and student)—repetition and feedback. Earlier, a similar concept was developed at the University of Tübingen by Zifreund (1966), which consisted of background knowledge transfer, first and second attempts, video recordings, feedback from supervisors, and training groups. The training was based on the extensive self-organization and self-responsibility of the participants, who were organized into small groups of four to six people, which is one of the main differences compared to the training concept at Stanford.

## 11.2 Components of a microteaching training program

Practical exercises in the laboratory, therefore, make an important contribution to the acquisition of effective behaviors and thus help improve the professional behavioral repertoire. Practical exercises with feedback can also be combined with other methods to create a specific training program. Effective programs include clear areas of knowledge and competence required for the acquisition and development of effective communication skills and abilities for interaction-intensive professions. These include the following five skills (Klinzing, 2002; Klinzing & Floden, 1991):

- The ability to use background knowledge
- The ability to use conceptual structures of interaction processes to analyze and guide action
- The ability to generate hypotheses

- The ability to perform actions appropriately
- The ability to learn from the effects (reflection)

### 11.1.1 The ability to use and analyze theoretical background knowledge

Theoretical background knowledge forms an initial frame of reference for the objectives, content, planning, and implementation of the training. Essential aids for deepening or acquiring knowledge are usually readings, lectures, discussions, and educational videos from the internet.

Pure knowledge, insights, and attitudes do not, of course, lead to a change in behavior. People often do not behave according to the insights they have expressed. Nevertheless, imparting theoretical background knowledge is a central initial component of training. A link must be established between the acquired knowledge and practice, which has a positive effect on practice. The target behaviors to be acquired relate to well-founded content.

### 11.1.2 The ability to use conceptual structures of interaction processes for analysis and orientation

Terms help us organize and analyze communicative situations. Relevant terms create a clear idea for teaching and communication strategies. Terms also help us analyze and find new possibilities for action. The use of key terms in feedback is extremely helpful. To acquire conceptual structures for organizing, analyzing, and implementing interactions, it is important to acquire action-guiding concepts. Model demonstration and observation training are important methods for acquiring such conceptual structures. Model demonstrations can be short films, videos, or written descriptions with positive or negative examples of the behavior to be developed.

Studies have shown that model demonstrations and the use of observation techniques in conjunction with background knowledge can effectively build up and support clear ideas about how to act in interaction situations (Cruickshank & Metcalf, 1990; Klinzing & Tisher, 1993). Of course, this is only one building block for the acquisition of effective behavior. It must also be possible to perform these behaviors in practical exercises in a qualified manner. This is all the more important when complex behaviors are involved. The target behaviors for interactive lecturing and adaptive teaching are very complex and are systematically developed in this course with the help of model demonstrations. This is also practiced by asking the course participants to give feedback on the target behaviors after the practical exercises and to identify them. Everyone is asked to independently develop alternatives and variations to the target behaviors. General feedback, such as "You're great" or "You did a great job," should be used only at the beginning or end. After that, the focus should be on discussing specific target behaviors.

### 11.1.3 The ability to form hypotheses and make decisions

Providing background knowledge, a clear idea of the target behavior, backed up by conceptual structures and implementation in the form of practical exercises in the laboratory and feedback are central aspects of microteaching. Reducing the complexity of the target behavior in the lab is helpful. Quick and targeted feedback is also possible in the laboratory, which can be implemented better there than in normal working life. The opportunity to repeatedly perform and analyze the behavior, try out alternative behaviors as strategies, and observe the consequences can also help develop new behaviors as a routine. Once specific teaching and interaction behaviors have been identified, the current situation can be related to theoretical background knowledge.

Concepts can be used to evaluate the actions performed and their consequences. If terms are used in addition to instructions for action, they can be linked to clear and concrete ideas about the associated behavior. This creates new possibilities and scope for generating hypotheses and thus new promising options for action. Hypotheses form a bridge between the knowledge-based analysis of the situation and the behavior to be performed. In an interaction situation, however, we must also repeatedly make decisions about the overall process of the interaction. It may be necessary to choose the most successful one to master the situation.

With the help of simulations, case studies, or "critical incidents," hypothesis formation and decision-making can be practiced. These methods are aimed at actively dealing with given situations. It is necessary to identify the problem, develop hypotheses to arrive at a solution, and make decisions about the best course of action. This process depends on the complexity of the problems to be solved. To work effectively with simulations, case studies, or critical incidents, background knowledge and the ability to analyze a situation are required. It is also important to have a large behavioral repertoire for implementation and evaluation. All of the methods mentioned above can help develop the ability to form hypotheses and make decisions.

### 11.1.4 The ability to perform actions properly

Actions should be carried out appropriately through practical, controlled practice, and with the help of microteaching. Individual teaching skills are related to the desired teaching situation or to another interactive situation (in the training described here, to interactive presentation and adaptive teaching). To make this possible, an initial test is carried out in relation to selected phases of the training program with subsequent feedback based on video recordings. A second test is then carried out, which includes the phases already shown in the first test with additional new phases of the training program, and feedback is again given on the basis of the video recordings. In the second feedback phase, the improvements from the first to the second attempt are specifically analyzed.

If you choose this procedure for a group that is to undergo training, it is important to delete the video recordings after each feedback session. Do not keep any video recordings. The past is the past. Orient yourself to the new target behavior. Microteaching is not a method for monitoring and controlling people. The aim is to expand the existing behavioral repertoire with effective behaviors, learn new behaviors if necessary, become aware of existing effective behaviors, or further refine and improve them. The aim of the training is not to reinforce inappropriate or ineffective behavior; these behaviors belong to the past.

### 11.1.5 Feedback in relation to specific effective skills

Feedback plays a central role in the acquisition of knowledge, the practice of conceptual structures, the development of clear ideas about target behavior, decision-making, and the analysis of instructions for action with the help of model demonstrations or observation training. Without the ability to reflect on these processes, effective and appropriate use is not possible, and the productive development of communicative competence in interactions does not occur. Feedback helps to reflect on the effects of actions and their execution. Feedback relates to specific target behaviors.

CHAPTER 12

# Effectiveness and appropriateness in the acquisition of behaviors and skills

Effectiveness and appropriateness are two important characteristics in the acquisition of communicative skills for interaction processes and interaction-intensive situations, which are always necessary when instructing, teaching, and mediating. Appropriateness refers to using the right skills to the right extent, at the right time, in the right way, and for the right purpose. Effectiveness is defined here as a skill that helps achieve a goal. Appropriateness means being able to cope with many different (teaching) situations and methods. Dealing with many different situations and (teaching) methods is also a maturing process. The more often a (similar) situation is experienced, the sooner (provided you have reflected on the respective situations) you learn to deal with it. It can also be described as "trial and error." However, this approach has the disadvantage of taking too long to acquire appropriate skills. Microteaching aims to shorten this acquisition period.

Microteaching is therefore an opportunity to practice and learn about specific teaching and learning situations. This takes place in a laboratory situation. It provides the opportunity to practice a specific situation in a protected environment. It is not important that mistakes are made or that certain situations are not mastered immediately; what is important is that we learn from these situations. However, the reflection of the mistakes must be related to effective target behaviors and competencies; otherwise, it is very difficult to learn from it. The next important step is to change the behavior that has been identified as ineffective. This is where the problem begins. Behaviors are very stable and sometimes difficult to change. However, well-designed and well-structured microteaching training programs, in which the individual training components are interrelated as described above, and which provide specific target behaviors and skills, help to pave the way for behavioral change. Appropriateness also includes the ability to comply with and respect the norms that apply to a situation in an interaction. Effective and appropriate skills in communicative situations are crucial for success.

# CHAPTER 13

# The selection of behavioral dimensions

To develop the content and skills for a training program, it is important to define, describe, and summarize the essential overarching components and dimensions. The dimensions determine the content, the associated behaviors, and skills for the training program interactive presentation and adaptive teaching of technical content. Behavioral dimensions serve as criteria for evaluating and categorizing these interactions (Argyle, 2017; Rupp, 1998) and for developing the ability to act in complex situations.

Adaptive teaching and learning do not use one approach or one form of teaching for learners. Adaptive teachers assess, for example, the different abilities of learners in a course or seminar. The requirements for teachers to use adaptation when imparting knowledge include the dimensions of variation and flexibility mentioned by Corno (2008), supplemented by the dimension of evaluation/assessment.

Table 35: Behavioral dimensions for training

| Behavioral dimensions | Important for |
|---|---|
| Variation | Contextual factors and variation in teaching methods |
| Flexibility | Processes in terms of procedure and relationship |
| Evaluation | Assessment, tests, feedback |

# CHAPTER 14

# The contents of the training program

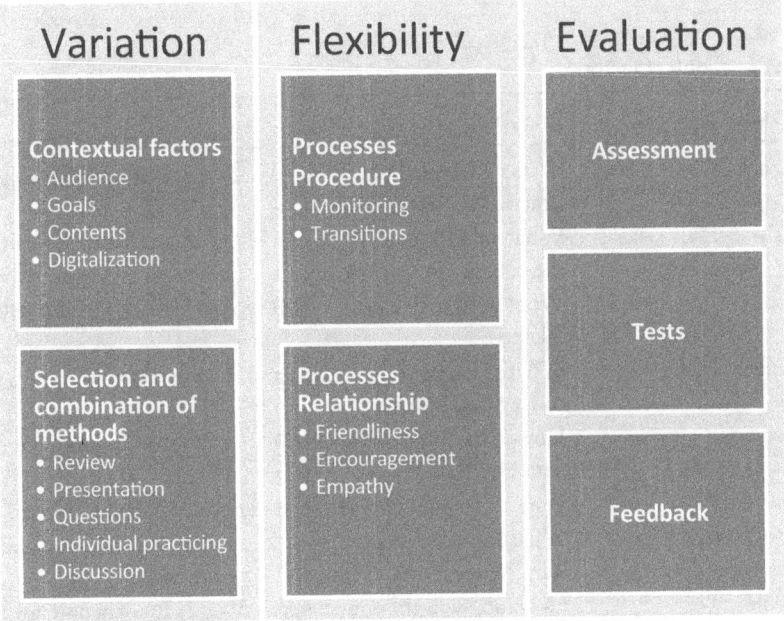

## 14.1 Dimension variation

The variation comprises two sub-dimensions: the context factors and the methods. The context factors sub-dimension refers to all aspects relating to the organization of the seminar/course as well as the learning time and the necessary media. The organization of a course or seminar is always dependent on the external framework conditions. As the external framework conditions are too diverse, there are no specific recommendations here. The learning time depends on the scope of the content that needs to be conveyed and the time allocated for this (e.g., in the curriculum). The sub-dimension of methods refers to different methods that are suitable for interactive presentation and adaptive teaching.

### 14.1.1 Context factors for planning

When planning interactive and adaptive teaching, it is important to consider both the individual and the specific group to whom the subject content is being taught, so that you can react flexibly to the respective situation. The factors shown in the table below must be taken into account when planning the selection, weighting, and sequence of content and information.

Table 36: Context factors

| Contextual factors | Important for |
| --- | --- |
| Audience | Who will attend the course? What are their backgrounds, experiences, and goals? |
| Goals | What should the participants know or achieve at the end of the course? |
| Contents | What topics are covered in the course? What content will be selected? |
| Resources | What resources (e.g., videos and literature) are necessary to convey these topics? |
| Format | How is the course conducted? In person, online, or a combination of both? |
| Digitalization | Which learning platform and digital tools are available? |
| Place of learning | What rooms and learning locations are available? Are there learning locations outside the institution? |
| Schedule | How long will the course take? What is the schedule for the individual units? |

## 14.1.2 Selection and combination of methods

For this training, five phases, which contain different methods and procedures, are selected and combined for the systematic practice of specific behaviors and skills for the training program. The five phases are based on the Rosenshine and Stevens (1986) model of "Direct Instruction" and the adapted and expanded approach of the microteaching courses of instruction by Rupp and Klinzing (1999, 2008) and Rupp (2021). The selected phases are described in detail in terms of the purpose of the phase, effective behaviors and skills, and exercises developed to practice them. In all phases, further variations can be integrated. For example, even more interactive options can be used for Phase 2. Phases 3 and 4 can be supplemented by a problem-oriented task, for example.

The five phases of interactive and adaptive content delivery are according to Rosenshine and Stevens (1986).

### PHASE 1: REVIEW/BEGINNING

Purpose of this phase: Regular repetitions serve to clarify errors/misunderstandings and to learn or refresh important areas of the content that have not been understood or retained. Repetitions serve to check whether your own progress as a teacher is not too fast or too slow.

Types of play for review, repetition, clarification of misunderstandings, corrections

- Repetition of the content and central concepts in the form of a presentation
- Questions about central concepts or basic skills
- Brief review (written or verbal) of the contents of the last training course(s)
- Repetition of the content in small groups (2–4 people) (e.g., with worksheets)

### EXERCISE

Please find more ways to review, repeat, and clarify misunderstandings.

## Phase 2: Interactive Presentation and Demonstration of New Content

Purpose of this phase: To introduce and present new content and to arouse interest and motivation.

Clarity, memorability, interest and motivation are important when presenting new content. Other important behaviors and skills are described in detail in Chapters 4 and 5. For this training, the important communicative behaviors described below are specifically selected from these chapters. The use of these skills significantly improves the presentation and is important for conveying new content. The behaviors mentioned here have different functions in the transfer of knowledge. They also help to create a better structure, consolidate and deepen knowledge, and arouse interest and motivation.

A. Selection of skills for clarity and memorability of the presentation

(i) *Provide an overview*
The brief presentation of the main contents of the presentation, the disclosure of the outline, offers a focus for the audience; it directs their thoughts and attention to the train of thought of the presentation, its main points, and their connection.

(ii) *Use of diverse examples*
Examples are used to relate as yet unknown information, terms, etc. to the existing knowledge, background experience, etc. of the audience (this is particularly effective if the examples are chosen from the experience/knowledge background of the audience).

(iii) *Use of analogies (from the experience of those present)*
An analogy is a comparison between two things that are different but have similarities in certain aspects or characteristics.

(iv) *Summary of contributions*
The contribution of a participant is summarized, and the important points are presented again for everyone.

(v) *Summary at the end of the presentation*
In a summary at the end of a presentation, the information is presented in a condensed form, the core of the information, and the main train of thought is presented again.

## (vi) *Proceed step by step*

The knowledge is presented step by step in a very detailed, highly structured way. All steps are of great importance; otherwise, the content may not be understood or applied to certain problems in the future. A step-by-step approach is suitable for scientific subjects.

## (vii) *Use of visualizations*

Illustrations and visualizations have several functions, including helping with retention, creating links to already existing knowledge, and facilitating the understanding of difficult-to-understand complex facts by illustrating as well as organizing and structuring the content.

## (viii) *Structuring*

Structural supports are hints and aids that make the structure/organization/thought process of a presentation explicit for those present.

## (ix) *Checking whether the information has been understood*

By asking the audience questions, it is possible to check whether all the content of the presentation has been understood and whether the main points and the main train of thought have been retained. If such questions are asked systematically, they have the effect of restructuring the content.

> **EXERCISE**
>
> Please assign the skills mentioned to the following two groups:
> (1) Formation of a structure or (2) improvement of memorization and practice (consolidation of knowledge).

### B. Arouse motivation and interest

When presenting new content, it is important to attract attention, arouse interest, and show enthusiasm (see Chapter 5 for details). Attention and/or interest should be generated through the use and variation of various means. This is mainly used at the beginning of a lesson or a new section. Possible means include:

- Visualization (see Chapter 8 for details)
- Audio
- Computer simulation
- Live demonstration

- Video (YouTube movies)
- Unique images
- Panel pictures
- Challenging questions
- Provocative questions (the question does not have to be followed by a correct answer)
- Humorous remarks

When presenting content, both verbal and non-verbal levels are important. Show enthusiasm through non-verbal behavior.

### C. Enthusiasm

Once the curiosity of those present has been aroused, it is important to use this momentum and show enthusiasm by varying posture, eye contact, voice, and gestures.

- Posture (appropriate, functional movement toward those present)
- Eye contact (eyes go to the person you are talking to, have everyone in view)
- Voice (variations and changes in the voice)
- Gestures (functional and expressive)

A detailed description of non-verbal behavior can be found in Chapter 7.

> **EXERCISE**
>
> Find other means of visualizing the information or data being communicated.

> ## PHASE 3: PRACTICING TOGETHER THROUGH QUESTIONS AND FEEDBACK REACTIONS TO ANSWERS
>
> Purpose of this phase: Guided practice in a controlled situation in which it is possible to correct mistakes.
> Checking whether the material has been understood and can be moved on to the next step, or whether part of the material needs to be repeated. Practice is stimulated and guided by questions/prompts with feedback reactions or corrections. Questions and probes are one way of supporting the learning process. The participants should think about the material presented, work with it and, if necessary, carry out an action.

## A. Practicing together

Oral practice is carried out by:

- close-ended questions,
- open-ended questions, or
- probing questions.

You can use close-ended questions. Close-ended questions are characterized having a single or limited number of correct answers. An example of this is: "What is 20 divided by 5?"

Open-ended questions, by contrast, can have several correct answers and cannot be answered with one word or statement. An example of this is "What does the term 'democracy' mean to you?"

Probing questions can be used for specific follow-up questions or to deepen the answers. These can then be "why questions," for example, if you want to explore a concept or answer it in more depth. An example of this is: "Why is the 'democracy' form of government important?" Clarifying and expanding behaviors can be used to go deeper. The teacher asks an individual in the audience to "clarify, deepen, or re-formulate" the answer, as the teacher wants to better understand what has been said. The teacher tries to expand on the answers by asking the students to add more information. An example of this is, "Are there any other examples of what was said?"

---

### EXERCISE: CLOSE-ENDED OR OPEN-ENDED QUESTIONS.

Please classify the following questions as closed (G) or open (O):
• What is the name of the capital of France?
• Why are presentations often so boring?
• What significance did Paris have for Europe in the Middle Ages?
• Name four different levels of feedback that have already been addressed in this course!
• What are the dimensions of the "Interactive adaptive teaching" model?
• What is the importance of communication in teaching?
• Do you have any ideas on how the studies at the university can be improved?
• What is your opinion on the introduction of new tests at the university?
• What functions do broad questions probably have in discussions?
• Please list the advantages of "Interactive Adaptive Teaching" as they have been explained in this course!

## B. Feedback reactions to answers

When practicing specific content, the teacher's feedback on the answers is also important. Practice should proceed quickly and rapidly. Use the "momentum." Lingering too long on individual items is not intended here. In the table, possible feedback reactions of the teacher to answers are formulated so that the "momentum" can be maintained.

According to Borich (2015), different types of student responses require distinct feedback strategies to enhance learning effectively.

1. For complete and correct answers that are provided quickly and confidently, clear affirmations such as "yes, correct" or "good" are appropriate.
2. When students give correct but hesitant or partially justified answers, the teacher should re-explain the content or pose probing questions to guide students to the correct solution.
3. If a student's response is partly incorrect but contains some accurate elements, the teacher should correct the errors and, if necessary, ask a follow-up question or redirect the question to other students.
4. For answers that are wrong due to knowledge gaps or if the student indicates they do not know, the teacher should provide the correct answer, offer hints to lead to the correct solution, or reteach the content.
5. If a student does not respond at all, the teacher should continue teaching and ensure the content is understood.

### EXERCISE: FEEDBACK REACTIONS

Please assign the appropriate feedback reactions to the answers. Please formulate the feedback reactions in literal speech. (In some situations, several possible answers are appropriate.)

Example 1
We have discussed the underlying principles of an explanation or instruction. Could you name them again?
Answer: Create a clear structure and presentation of knowledge. Proceed step by step, linking with what is already known, practicing the knowledge so that it becomes available.
(The answer will be given completely, correctly, and confidently.)
Please formulate your feedback reactions.

Example 2
How does the model presented here do justice to these principles?

Answer: Practicing happens, ... uh, ... material is presented clearly, then I think there's something with small steps and ... uh, ... don't forget the link.
(The answer is partially correct but hesitant and uncertain.)
Please formulate your feedback reactions.

Example 3
What is the function of closed questions?
Answer: Questions create a clear structure.
(The answer is wrong, but this is just a careless mistake)
Please formulate your feedback reactions.

Example 4
What does it mean if only 30–40% of the questions are answered correctly?
Answer: That the subject matter has been understood correctly.
(The answer is wrong and is given due to gaps in knowledge or faulty thought processes).
Please formulate your feedback reactions.

Example 5
You want to apply the "adaptive teaching" model in the classroom. Explain the main dimensions of the model!
Answer: You will not receive an answer
Please formulate your feedback reactions.

## PHASE 4: INDIVIDUAL PRACTICE (INDIVIDUALLY, WITH TWO PEOPLE OR IN SMALL GROUPS/BUZZ GROUPS)

Purpose of Phase 4: Automation of the new knowledge (so that it is no longer necessary to think through every step in solving the tasks). Consolidation of the new content by the participants themselves.

Once everyone has gained some confidence with the new content (i.e., has answered approximately 80% of the questions in Phase 3 correctly), the phase of individual practice begins. This usually takes place as "silent work" in pairs or in small groups based on worksheets or instructions. The following procedure has proven to be successful in implementing this phase. You start with individual work first, then after a certain amount of time (depending on the amount of work to be done), you move on to working in pairs or small groups. The purpose of this approach is to allow time to absorb and process the information before working in pairs or in small groups to deepen the content, clarify problems, and allow for mutual questioning.

1. Tasks and skills before practicing
   - Create exercise material (provide assistance with the procedure for learning the material or task).
   - Give clear instructions on the tasks before the individual practice begins.
   - Introduce rules that should be applied during individual practice, for example, how to get help, what to do when someone has finished practicing, and allow enough time to practice the tasks successfully.

2. Tasks and skills during practice
   - The teacher goes from group member to group member and supervises the work but always keeps an eye on everyone (monitoring). Feedback is given, process questions are asked, and if necessary, brief explanations or help are given. The contacts with the individual persons are short (30 seconds to 1 minute). If longer contacts are necessary, the explanation of the new material and its practice was not detailed or good enough.

3. Pair/small-group work
   - Mutual help also takes place when working in pairs or in small groups and is encouraged. This not only achieves social goals, such as cooperation, but also deepens the subject content by exchanging information. Groups can be formed by the teacher with the aim of further improving the social interaction between individual group members.

### EXERCISE

What tasks and skills do teachers need to plan and consider before the individual practice phase?

What tasks and skills do teachers need to plan and take into account during the individual practice phase?

### PHASE 5: DEEPENING THROUGH DISCUSSION

Purpose of phase 5: Consolidation of the information presented and the results achieved individually or in small groups. This increases the acquisition of the learning material and improves retention. Discussion is also suitable for improving social behavior, acquiring social skills, changing attitudes and positively experiencing and using social interactions in a group. See Section 9.8 for more details.

1. Tasks at the beginning of the discussion
   - The aim is to bring all participants to a level of information that allows them to participate in the discussion in a truly informed manner. The starting point is the content conveyed in the previous phases. Only after this are discussions effective! If the topic is new, it must be developed in other forms (lecture, reading, individual or partner work, films, videos) before it can be discussed.
   - Even if the content foundations have been laid out, it is advisable to recall the key content again in a brief introduction at the start of the discussion.
   - Introduction to the content of the discussion: Introduce the actual discussion through a broad, open initial question.
   - The introduction to the topic and the initial question must be clear and precise. Unclear introductions and unclear questions do not lead to a deepening of the content but to a discussion of what should actually be discussed.
   - State the aim of the discussion.

2. Tasks during the discussion
   The process must be closely monitored during the discussion and, if necessary, supported by the following measures:
   - Initiating and stimulating content-related contributions
   - Structuring the content of the discussion
   - Providing assistance in expressing or developing the thoughts of individual discussion participants
   - Ensuring that the content and form of the contributions are correct

3. Tasks at the end of the discussion
   - Summarize the most important results.
   - Ask someone from the group to summarize the results.
   - Write a backup of the results of the discussion, if necessary.

---

### EXERCISE

Formulate a clear, precise, open question to start a discussion.

## 14.2 Dimension flexibility

The flexibility dimension comprises the sub-dimension of sequential processes and the interpersonal processes of teaching. This includes monitoring the transitions to different activities and the organization of the relationship between the individuals and the group as a whole. Effective teachers take into account the different abilities of individuals in a course/seminar.

When carrying out the various phases described above, the teacher needs to be flexible. Good and successful teachers value the diversity of talents in the seminar/course. Good teaching does not use one approach or arrangement for all. The behaviors of the flexibility dimension include monitoring/observation, transitions, and relationships with individuals and groups.

### 14.2.1 Monitoring

An important behavior to engage students in the learning process involves monitoring and review. It is the ability to perceive many, if not all, aspects simultaneously during teaching. The teacher observes more than one activity in the course. Kounin (1976) described this ability as "withitness," which means nothing other than "omnipresence." Teachers literally have "eyes in the back of the head." Since we don't have them, other ways are necessary to show the "omnipresence" during the lesson.

> **EXERCISE**
>
> Find behaviors that, in your opinion, express the omnipresence of the teacher toward the students. In each case for the verbal and non-verbal level.

### 14.2.2 Transitions

- Efficient switching between different activities
- Maintaining attention
- Formulate clear expectations regarding behavior

Transitions describe the efficient change of different activities that are necessary within a lesson or project. Evertson and Emmer (2013) showed that it is difficult to switch from an instructive task, such as a lecture or discussion, to an organizational (non-instructive) task, such as handing out documents or materials, without losing a lot of time. However, it is not only the time that is lost but also the students' attention. There may also be interruptions over which you have no control (e.g., external disruptions). Less effective teachers have great difficulty keeping the attention of the pupils, in contrast to effective teachers.

These include, for example, moving from a presentation to silent work, from a discussion to an explanation, or from a presentation to a discussion. The problems during these transitions are created for two reasons: a lack of readiness on the part of the learner to perform the next activity and unclear expectations regarding appropriate behavior during the transition.

## EXERCISE

Effective behaviors for problems during a transition in a task-oriented activity.
Please formulate instructions/measures for the situations mentioned here in literal speech.

1. Students are loud at the beginning of the transition:
   Instructions/measures:
2. Students band together during the transition to prevent the start of the next activity.
   Instructions/measures:
3. Individual students finish their tasks before the required time and disturb others.
   Instructions/measures:
4. Students continue to work on the previous activity after the change.
   Instructions/measures:
5. For some students, the completion of the activity is delayed compared to the other students.
   Instructions/measures:

Possible solutions
1. The teacher establishes a rule that talking is not allowed between transitions, recognizing that it is difficult to tolerate/allow a certain level of noise and leave it at that.
2. The teacher does not allow/give more time than is necessary for the necessary activity. For example, clearing away documents, fetching/providing new material.
3. The teacher has prepared additional tasks to fill in the free time.
4. The teacher gives information before the end of the task: 5 minutes left, 2 minutes left, etc. using verbal statements, such as "We will be finishing shortly," then carries on.
   Make the end of the task clear: This is the end of the activity.

5. The teacher does not wait for those who delay the process. When the next natural break comes, talk to the students and make them aware that they need to stop now and move on to the next activity. They recognize what it is: lack of motivation, material not prepared, distracting activities.

### 14.2.3 Relationship with individuals and the group

A productive mutual relationship with individuals and the group as a whole is crucial for cognitive processes and mutual cooperation. This is achieved through kindness, encouragement, and empathy on both verbal and non-verbal levels.

#### A. Friendliness

- Friendliness has many possible forms of expression and facets, including very different psychological characteristics, such as consideration, understanding, emotionality, and affirmation. Watzlawick et al. (1985) considered affirmation to be the most important prerequisite for a person's mental stability and development. For us, kindness is always associated with something big and universal, as feelings are triggered. Kindness also plays a major role in students. In addition, it has a positive effect on cognitive processes and mutual cooperation (Tausch & Tausch, 1998). Kindness also means showing an understanding of a situation in which someone finds themselves.
- Friendliness is demonstrated during lessons in the following ways, among others:
  - Welcoming and saying goodbye to those present as an act of attentiveness
  - Chatting during the break.
  - A friendly choice of words, for example, "I am pleased that you are here." "I look forward to working with you for the next few hours."
  - Non-verbal behavior, such as "smiling" when greeting someone and eye contact when speaking or listening.

> **EXERCISE**
>
> Formulate other acts of kindness toward students in a teaching situation.

B. Encouragement
- Encouraging behavior on the part of the teacher can make a very positive contribution to the overall mood in a course. Encouraging behavior has a positive influence on cognitive processes and on the cooperative behavior of students. It also promotes mutual helpfulness and increases the ability to solve tasks and problems creatively. Positive effects can also be observed in terms of motivation and interpersonal relationships.
- Encouragement is shown during lessons in the following ways, among others:
  - Encouraging someone to concretize a contribution.
  - Encouraging someone to speak up.
  - Encouraging statements that suggest a problem will soon be solved.

**EXERCISE**

Formulate other acts of encouragement toward students in a teaching situation.

C. Empathy
- Empathy is the ability to participate in the experiences of others and put oneself cognitively and emotionally in another person's shoes (DeVito, 1982). Empathy is demonstrated, for example, through active listening and verbal responses that make it clear that one understands the feelings and situations of the other person. Empathy is demonstrated during lessons in the following ways, among others:
  - Expression of attitudes and values on a topic.
  - Take responsibility for your own feelings and thoughts.
  - Reflection of feelings.

**EXERCISE**

Formulate further acts of empathy toward students in a teaching situation.

## 14.3 Dimension evaluation

The evaluation dimension includes assessment, tests, and feedback. Black and William (2004) distinguished between formative and summative assessments, with the former referring to the evaluation of the learning process and the latter the evaluation of what has been learned as summative.

Teaching also includes evaluating learners' performance. This can be at the beginning of the course or at the end, and includes three main features that partly overlap in terms of the timing or the way in which these forms of evaluation are used.

### 14.3.1 Assessment

An individual's qualifications are determined at the institutional level. This proof of achievement can be a certificate (e.g., university entrance qualification) to gain access to an institution, the successful completion of a preliminary course, for example, in mathematics, to gain a place at university, a language test (e.g., TOEFL test) to be able to take part in a semester of study abroad or the successful completion of an assessment center. Within the European and international framework, the recognition of qualifications is regulated and organized by the ENIC-NARIC networks (European Network of Information Centres (ENIC) in the European Region and National Academic Recognition Information Centres (NARIC) in the European Union). The European Qualifications Framework (EQF) is a qualifications framework that works with 8 levels. The EQF is intended to ensure transparency in the EU and to make the various qualifications in the EU comparable. At the seminar or course level, for example, competences or skills can be assessed by means of a questionnaire or an entrance test. At the seminar or course level, for example, various competencies or skills can be assessed using a questionnaire or an entrance test. The two questionnaires for the assessment of communicative skills in relation to expressiveness and participant orientation (Self-rated Competence [SRC] and Rating of Alter Competence [RAC]) are suitable for this approach (Spitzberg, 1988).

The reliability and validity of the questionnaire are high, as not only is the respondent's own assessment of communicative behavior collected, but this finding is verified by the assessment of third parties.

### 14.3.2 Tests, examinations, and certificates of achievement

Effective teachers see the individual differences of learners both within and between learners in the continuous process of teaching in relation to specific events during the lesson but also outside the curriculum. One way to account for individual differences is to create meaningful subgroups at the outset based on experiences with particular learners from a large group. Opportunities to assess qualifications can be carried out at the beginning, during, or at the end of the lesson or learning unit in summative testing (assessment of learning) or in formative testing (assessment of the learning process).

Examples of summative tests

1. Name five personality traits that you can use to describe heterogeneity in a group.
2. Which social changes play a central role in the concept of diversity? Name three terms and explain them.
3. What measures are suitable in the classroom to compensate for socio-economic differences?
4. What dimensions does the concept of adaptive teaching include?
5. How can you use the flexibility dimension for teaching?
6. How can you create attention at the beginning of a lesson? Name four possibilities.
7. What behavior can you use to create a structure among students?
8. What non-verbal behaviors can you use to generate enthusiasm when presenting?
9. Define the term "close question" and give an example.
10. Define the term "broad question" and give an example.
11. What feedback do you give when a student's answer is "correct, fast, complete, and secure."
12. What tasks and skills must the teacher take into account before planning the individual practice phase?
13. How does friendliness (on the behavioral level) show itself during the lesson? Please give two examples.
14. Please formulate a "process feedback" in literal speech.

### EXERCISE

Design a summative test:
Design a formative test:

## 14.3.3 Feedback, praise, and recognition

Feedback is one of the most effective features of successful teaching. It is extremely variable in application and reduces the perception gaps between "where you are" and "where you think you are." It helps to focus the learner on the success of a task, provides information about ideas that have not been understood, motivates them to invest more in the task or skill, restructures and improves their understanding of their own cognitive processes, points them in a direction in which they can go, and shows them alternatives. Feedback is necessary because mistakes arise and are made (this is not a deficit; mistakes are necessary). Effective feedback can be concretized with three questions: What is the goal of the efforts? How do you make progress with your efforts? What comes next? All of these feedback questions can be applied to the four levels of feedback (Hattie, 2013). Feedback should provide information about the task. Feedback is one effective skill among many others. Feedback must also be clear, targeted, and consistent with the learner's prior knowledge and must focus on the task, process, and regulation, not on the learner's own *self*.

### A. Four levels of feedback (Hattie, 2013)

| Feedback levels | Important for |
| --- | --- |
| Task/product level | Execution of the task |
| Process level | Strategies and processes to understand the task |
| Self-regulation level | Recognize your own learning process |
| Personal level | Own personal assessment |

Task/product level: Refers to how well the task was performed and whether a task is correct or incorrect.

- Refers to the task or product
- The most common type of feedback in educational institutions
- The task is correct or incorrect
- Often given in response to questions from the teacher
- It is often specifically geared toward a task or a product
- Further differentiated answers are requested

## Exercise

Please formulate examples in literal speech for feedback at the task/product level.

Process level: Refers to the strategies required to perform a task and whether there are alternative strategies.

- Leads to alternative solutions
- Reduces cognitive overload
- Helps to develop learning strategies
- Keyword to find an even better answer
- Helps to understand connections between thoughts and ideas
- Helps identify strategies to explicitly learn from mistakes
- Helps to gain a better understanding of the subject matter

## Exercise

Please formulate examples in literal speech for feedback at the process level.

Self-regulation level: Refers to the knowledge needed to understand what one is doing and how to complete a task.

- Focuses on the learner's own learning process
- Shows confidence in the ability to work even harder on a task
- Supports the acceptance of feedback
- Supports the search for feedback

## Exercise

Please formulate examples in literal speech for feedback at the process level.

Personal level: Refers to the improvement of one's own assessment

- Shows possibilities for self-evaluation
- Develops confidence in your own ability to continue learning
- Uses reflective questions, such as "Where am I? Why am I at this point?"

> **EXERCISE**
>
> Please formulate examples in literal speech for feedback on a personal level.

### B. Effective praise and recognition

Effective verbal recognition/praise increases intrinsic motivation, and learners spend more time on tasks (Hattie, 2013). Effective verbal praise is given immediately (manifested in spontaneity, variability, and other signs of credibility) and specifies the details of achievement. It is appropriate in expression, facial expression, gesture, and tone of voice and is always related to the contribution or matter. It is a guide for the learner to better self-assess his or her task-related behavior and problem-solving thinking, informing him or her about the value of the achievement, and acknowledging the great effort or success in a difficult task.

By contrast, ineffective recognition or praise is given randomly or unsystematically. It is given only in relation to performance improvement, has transparent uniformity, and rewards mere participation in a task without consideration of performance processes or results. It is only a guide to compare oneself with others and to stimulate competitive thinking and is given without regard to the effort put in and without regard to the significance of the performance for the person (cf. Brophy, 1979).

> **EXERCISE**
>
> Please praise an achievement in literal speech.

# CHAPTER 15

# Results of the training program

## 15.1 Results of the seminar evaluation questionnaire

The training program described here was evaluated using the German version of the Course/Instructor Evaluation Questionnaire (CIEQ) at the end of the training program (Klinzing & Rupp, 1989). The questionnaire consists of 21 statements rated on a four-point scale from "strongly agree" (1) to "strongly disagree" (4). The 21 questions measure five factors: general attitude toward the course, teaching-learning method, seminar content, interest, and attention (four questions each), and lecturer (five questions).

Table 37: Results of the seminar evaluation questionnaire

|  | N = 15 |
|---|---|
| General attitude toward the course | 1.56 |
| Teaching-learning method | 1.58 |
| Interest | 1.40 |
| Seminar contents | 1.35 |
| Trainer | 1.61 |

## 15.2 Results of the self- and alter competence questionnaire

In a pre- and post-test, the participants assessed themselves in terms of their communicative and social competence (expressiveness and participant orientation) in this training seminar using the German version of the Self-Rated Competence (SRC, 28 questions, 5-point scale). They were also assessed by their internship supervisors after their teaching units using the German version of the Rating of Alter Competence (RAC, 28 questions, 5-point scale).

Both questionnaires were developed by Cupach and Spitzberg (Spitzberg, 1988). The German version was adapted and translated by Rupp (1999), with the permission of Brian Spitzberg. In 11 studies, the determined reliability of the questionnaire (RAC) was between $r = .90$ and $r = .94$. The SRC questionnaire was tested for reliability in 11 studies with approximately 3,000 students. This was rated at $r = ...87$ and $r = ...92$ (Spitzberg, 1988).

The results showed differences between self-competence and alter competence and a slight increase in individual areas of competence.

Considering the results of the training program as a whole, it becomes clear that only a very small number of people performed worse. The participants who had already performed well continued to demonstrate effective behavior in a positive

Table 38: Results of the self- and alter competence questionnaire

| Variable | Pre-test | | Post-test | | | | |
|---|---|---|---|---|---|---|---|
| | x | S | x | S | t | p | ES |
| Self-competence—expressiveness | 3.60 | 0.4898486 | 3.85 | 0.5267341 | 0.2239 | 0.85 | 0.49 |
| Self-competence—participant orientation | 3.83 | 0.45919 | 4.11 | 0.5059101 | 0.13 | 0.91 | 0.61 |
| External competence—expressiveness | 4.29 | 0.51675924 | 4.49 | 0.4645220 | 0.0015 | 0.99 | 0.47 |
| External competence—participant orientation | 4.05 | 0.59248963 | 4.51 | 0.3316127 | 0.023 | 0.98 | 1 |

Comparison of pre-test and post-test, mean values, standard deviations, *t*-tests, effect sizes sense. The average performers improved, and the poor performers improved significantly. This shows a positive result for everyone.

## 15.3 Summary

The microteaching training program "Interactive and adaptive teaching of subject content" presented here was developed with reference to the elements described above have been developed, successfully implemented, and evaluated. The frame of reference and the underlying concept enable the development of training programs on a scientific basis. It is also based on the assumption that various areas of knowledge and skills can only fully generate effective and appropriate actions in communicative situations when they interact with each other. Through the targeted arrangement of specific, scientifically tested training modules, an increase and measurable continuous improvement of competencies and specific skills can be achieved.

This microteaching training program is therefore suitable for the acquisition of skills and behaviors in various communicative situations, as well as for the use of other (teaching) methods that are necessary, for example, for imparting or transferring knowledge or changing attitudes. The training program is therefore suitable for anyone who wants to review, expand, and improve their own repertoire of communicative (teaching) behaviors or who is also looking for opportunities to apply new behaviors in other teaching (methods) or communicative situations.

# Bibliography

Adelswärd, I., & Öberg, B. M. (1998). The function of laughter and joking in negotiation activities. *Humor, 11*(4), 411–430. https://doi.org/10.1515/humr.1998.11.4.411

Allen, D. W., & Ryan, K. A. (1969). *Microteaching*. Addison-Wesley.

Allodi, M. W. (2010). The meaning of social climate of learning environments: Some reasons why we do not care enough about it. *Learning Environments Research, 13*(2), 89–104. https://doi.org/10.1007/s10984-010-9072-9

Anderson, J. R. (2013). *Cognitive psychology* (7th ed.). Springer VS.

Argyle, M. (2017). *Social interaction: Process and products* (2nd ed.). Taylor & Francis.

Argyle, M., Furnham, A., & Graham, J. A. (1981). *Social situations*. Cambridge University Press.

Ausubel, D. P. (1974). *Psychology of teaching*. Beltz.

Barkley, E. F., & Mayor, C. H. (2018). *Interactive lecturing. A handbook for college faculty*. Jossey-Bass.

Barnett, J. (2006). Implementation of personal response units in very large lecture classes: Student perceptions. *Australasian Journal of Educational Technology, 22*(6), 474–494.

Bateson, G. (1985). *Ecology of the mind*. Suhrkamp.

Biggs, J. (1996). Enhancing teaching through constructive alignment. *Higher Education, 32*, 347–364.

Black, P. & William, D. (2004). The formative purpose: Assessment must first promote learning. *Yearbook of the Natioanl Society for the Study of Education, 103*, 20–50. http://dx.doi.org/10.1111/j.1744-7984.2004.tb00047.x

Bligh, D. A. (2000). *What's the use of lectures?* Jossey-Bass.

Bloom, B. S., Engelhart, M. D., Furst, E. J., Hill, W. J., & Krathwohl, D. R. (1956). *Taxonomy of educational objectives: The classification of educational goals. Handbook I: Cognitive domain.* Longmans.

Borich, G. (2015). *Observation skills for effective teaching* (7th ed.). Routledge.

Brekelmans, M., Mainhard, T., den Brok, P., & Wubbels, T. (2011). Teacher control and affiliation: Do students and teachers agree? *Journal of Classroom Interaction, 46*(1), 17–26.

Bridges, D. (1979). *Education, democracy and discussion.* Nelson.

Brophy, J. E. (1979). Teacher behavior and its effects. *Journal of Educational Psychology, 71*(6), 733–750. https://doi.org/10.1037/0022-0663.71.6.733

Burgoon, J., & Hale, J. (1984). The fundamental topoi of relational communication. *Communication Monographs, 51*, 193–214.

Buskist, W., & Keeley, J. W. (2018). Searching for universal principles of excellence in college and university teaching. *New Directions for Teaching and Learning. Special Issue: Habits and Practices of Master Teachers: International Perspectives on Excellent Teaching, 2018*(156), 95–105. https://doi.org/10.1002/tl.20321

Cain, J., Esther, P., Black, E. P., & Rohr, J. (2009). An audience response system strategy to improve student motivation, attention, and feedback. *American Journal of Pharmaceutical Education, 73*(2), 21, 1–7. https://doi.org/10.5688/aj730221

Chen, C.-H., Chen H.-C., & Roberts, A. M. (2019). Why humor enhances creativity from theoretical explanations to an empirical humor training program: Effective "Ha-Ha" helps people to "A-Ha." In S. R. Luria, J. Baer, & J. C. Kaufman (Eds.), *Humor and creativity* (Ch. 4, pp. 83–108). Academic Press. https://doi.org/10.1016/C2017-0-00003-4

Chilcoat, G. W. (1987). Teacher clarity in the middle school classroom: A functional review of research. *Middle School Research Selected Studies, 12*(1), 36–64. https://doi.org/10.1080/08851700.1987.11670279

Corno, L. (2008). On teaching adaptively. Educational Psychologist, 43(3), 161-173. https://doi.org/10.1080/00461520802178466

Cruickshank, D. R., Jenkins, D. B., & Metcalf, K. K. (2012). *The act of teaching* (6th ed.). McGraw-Hill.

Cruickshank, D. R., & Metcalf, K. K. (1990). Training within teacher preparation. In W. R. Houston (Ed.). *Handbook of research on teacher education* (pp. 469–497). Macmillian.

Dohn, N. B., Madsen, P. T., & Malte, H. (2009). The situational interest of undergraduate students in zoophysiology. *Advances in Physiology Education, 33*(3), 196–201. https://doi.org/10.1152/advan.00038.2009

DeVito, J. A. (1982). *Communicology: An introduction to the study of communication* (2nd ed.). Harper & Row.

Duarte, N. (2009). *Slide:ology.* O'Reilly.

Easton, G. (2016). How medical teachers use narratives in lectures: A qualitative study. *BMC Medical Education, 16*(1). https://doi.org/10.1186/s12909-015-0498-8

Ekman, P. (2004). *Reading emotions: How to recognize and correctly interpret emotions.* Elsevier.

Ellis, D. (2015, October 29–30). *Using Padlet to increase student engagement in lectures* [Paper presentation]. European Conference on eLearning (ECEL), Hatfield, UK.

Evertson, C. M., & Emmer, E. T. (2013). *Classroom management for elementary teachers.* (9th ed.). Pearson.

Fogelgarn, R., Burns, E., & Lewis, R. (2021). Hinting as a pedagogical strategy to promote prosocial behavior. *Educational Action Research, 29*(5), 755–777. https://doi.org/10.1080/09650792.2020.1743333

Freeman, S., Eddy, S. L., McDonough, M., Smith, M. K., Okoroafor, N., Jordt, H., & Wenderoth, M. P. (2014). Active learning increases student performance in science, engineering, and mathematics. *Proceedings of the National Academy of Sciences, 111*(23), 8410–8415. https://doi.org/10.1073/pnas.1319030111

Gage, N., & Berliner, D. C. (1996). *Educational psychology* (5th rev. ed.).

Gall, M. D. (1987). Discussion methods. In M. J. Dunkin (Ed.), *The international encyclopedia of teaching and teacher education* (pp. 232–237). Pergamon.

Grimm Brothers. (1812, 1857). *Hans in luck. Children's and household tales by the Brothers Grimm*, in the editions between 1812 and 1857. KHM 83. https://khm.li/Impressum

Goffman, E. (1971). *The presentation of self in everyday life.* Pelican Books.

Gregory, J. L. (2013). Lecture is not a dirty word: How to use active lecture to increase student engagement. *International Journal of Higher Education, 2*(4), 116–122. https://doi.org/10.5430/ijhe.v2n4p116

Hall, E. T. (1959). *The silent language.* Doubleday & Company.

Hall, E. T. (1976). *The language of space.* Pädagogischer Verlag Schwann.

Hall, E. T. (1990). *The silent language.* Anchor Books.

Hall, R. H., Collier, H. L., Thomas, M. L., & Hilgers, M. G. (2005). A student response system for increasing engagement, motivation, and learning in high enrollment lectures. *Eleventh Americas Conference on Information Systems, 2005; Omaha, NE, USA. AMCIS Proceedings, 255* (pp. 621–626). https://aisel.aisnet.org/amcis2005/255

Hattie, J. (2013). *Making learning visible.* Schneider Verlag.

Hewes, G. (1973). Primate communication and the gestural origin of language. *Current Anthropology, 14*, 5–24. https://doi.org/10.1086/201401

Hidi, S. (1990). Interest and its contribution as a mental source of learning. *Review of Educational Research, 60*(4), 549–571.

Hidi, S. (2001). Interest, reading, and learning: Theoretical and practical considerations. *Educational Psychology Review, 13*(3), 191–209.

Hiller, J. A., Fisher, G. A., & Kaess, W. (1969). A computer investigation of verbal characteristics of effective classroom lecturing. *American Educational Research Journal, 6*(4), 661–675.

Hofstadter, D., & Sander, E. (2014). *The analogy. The heart of thinking.* Klett-Cotta.

Jameson Boex, L. F. (2000). Attributes of effective economics instructors: An analysis of student evaluations. *The Journal of Economic Education, 31*(3), 211–227. https://doi.org/10.1080/00220480009596780

Jang, H., Reeve, J., & Deci, E. L. (2010). Engaging students in learning activities: It is not autonomy support or structure but autonomy support and structure. *Journal of Educational Psychology, 102*, 588–600. https://doi.org/10.1037/a0019682

Johnson, D. W., & Johnson, R. T. (1995). Goal structures. In L. W. Anderson (Ed.), *The international encyclopedia of teaching and teacher education* (pp. 349–359). Pergamon.

Johnson, D. W., & Johnson, R. T. (2018). Cooperative learning: The foundation for active learning. In S. M. Brito (Ed.), *Active learning, 5*, 1–12. https://doi.org/10.5772/inte-chopen.81086

Joyce, B., Weil, M., & Calhoun, E. (2014). *Models of teaching* (9th ed.). Pearson.

Kaiser, F. J., & Bretschneider, V. (2015). Case study. In J. Wiechman & S. Wildhirt (Eds.), *Twelve teaching methods*. Beltz.

Kay, R. H., & LeSage, A. (2009). Examining the benefits and challenges of using audience response systems: A review of the literature. *Computers & Education, 53*, 819–827. https://doi.org/10.1016/j.compedu.2009.05.001

Keller, M. M., Woolfolk Hoy, A. E., Goetz, T., & Frenzel, A. C. (2016). Teacher enthusiasm: Reviewing and redefining a complex construct. *Educational Psychology Review, 28*, 743–769. https://doi.org/10.1007/s10648-015-9354-y

Kelley, J. W., Ismail, E., & Buskist, W. (2016). Excellent teachers' perspectives on excellent teaching. *Teaching of Psychology, 43*(3), 175–179.

Klein, R., & Celik, T. (2017). *The wits intelligent teaching system: Detecting student engagement during lectures using convolutional neural networks* [Paper presentation]. IEEE International Conference on Image Processing (ICIP), Beijing, China. IEEE (pp. 2856–2860). https://doi.org/10.1109/ICIP.2017.8296804

Klinzing, H. G. (1998). Interacting as experimenting. In H. G. Klinzing (Ed.), *New learning methods: Second festschrift for Walter Zifreund* (pp. 231–341). dgvt-Verlag.

Klinzing, H. G. (2002). How effective is microteaching? A review of thirty-five years of research. *Journal of Education, 48*(2), 194–214.

Klinzing, H. G., & Floden, R. E. (1991). *The development of the micro-teaching in Europe.* [Paper presentation]. American Educational Research Association, Chicago, IL, United States.

Klinzing, H. G., & Rupp, A. (1989). CIEQ German version, translated and adapted for trainings. Adapted primarily from the Aleamoni Course/Instructor Evaluation Questionnaire (CIEQ). Results interpretation manual form 76 by L. M. Aleamoni (1975). Tucson, AZ: Office of Instructional Research and Development, University of Arizona. Adapted with permission.

Klinzing, H. G., & Tisher, R. P. (1993). The development of classroom teaching skills. In H. Vonk, L. Krem-Hayon, & R. Fessler (Eds.), *Teacher professional development* (pp. 167–196). Swets & Zeitlinger.

Kounin, J. S. (1976). *Techniques of classroom management*. Hans Huber.

Kroeber-Riel, W. (1996). *Image communication*. Vahlen.

Lewis, R. (2008). *Understanding pupil behavior. Classroom management techniques for teachers.* Routledge.

Lewis, R. (2023). *Obedience or responsibility: Why students don't misbehave. Implications for teachers.* IAMST International Association for Microteaching, Simulation and Training, Mössingen, Germany. Adapted and translated with permission. http://www.microteaching.eu

Mager, R. (1975). *Preparing instructional objectives* (2nd ed.). Fearon.

McKeachie, W. J. (1990). Research on college teaching: The historical background. *Journal of Educational Psychology, 82*(2), 189–200. https://doi.org/10.1037/0022-0663.82.2.189

Mehrabian, A. (1972). *Nonverbal communication.* Aldine.

Merseth, K. K. (1996). Cases and case methods in teacher education. In J. Sikula (Ed.), *Handbook of research on teacher education* (pp. 722–746). Macmillan.

Mueller, P. A., & Oppenheimer, D. M. (2014). The pen is mightier than the keyboard: Advantages of longhand over laptop note taking. *Psychological Science, 25*(6), 1159–1168. https://doi.org/10.1177/0956797614524581

Nir, N., & Halperin, E. (2019). Effects of humor on intergroup communication in intractable conflicts: Using humor in an intergroup appeal facilitates stronger agreement between groups and a greater willingness to compromise. *Political Psychology, 40*(3), 467–485. https://doi.org/10.1111/pops.12535

Nkomo, L. M., & Daniel, B. K. (2021). *Sentiment analysis of student engagement with lecture recording. TechTrends, 65,* 213–224. https://doi.org/10.1007/s11528-020-00563-8

Oliveira, P. C., & Oliveira, C. G. (2013). Using conceptual questions to promote motivation and learning in physics lectures. *European Journal of Engineering Education, 38*(4), 417–424. https://doi.org/10.1080/03043797.2013.780013

Provalis Research. (2024). *Communication vagueness dictionary.* https://provalisresearch.com/products/content-analysis-software/wordstat-dictionary/communication-vagueness-dictionary/

Randi, J., & Corno, L. (2005). Teaching and learner variation. In P. Tomlinson, J. Dockrell, & P. Winne (Eds.), *Pedagogy-teaching for learning* (pp. 47–69). British Psychological Society.

Reed, D. K., Rimel, H., & Hallett, A. (2016.) Note-taking interventions for college students: A synthesis and meta-analysis of the literature. *Journal of Research on Educational Effectiveness, 9*(3), 307–333. https://doi.org/10.1080/19345747.2015.1105894

Renninger, K. A. (1990). Children's play interests, representation, and activity. In R. Fivush & J. A. Hudson (Eds.), *Knowing and remembering in young children* (pp. 127–165). Cambridge University Press.

Renninger, K. A., & Hidi, S. (2011). Revisiting the conceptualization, measurement and generation of interest. *Educational Psychologist, 46*(3), 168–184. https://doi.org/10.1080/00461520.2011.587723

Reyes-Fournier, E., Cumella, E. J., March, M., Pederson, J., & Blackman, G. (2020). Development and validation of the online teaching effectiveness scale. *Online Learning, 24*(2), 111–127. https://doi.org/10.24059/olj.v24i2.2071

Rogers, C. R. (1983). *The client-centered conversation psychotherapy*. Fischer.

Rosenshine, B., & Stevens, R. (1986). Teaching functions. In M. C. Wittrock (Ed.), *Handbook of research on teaching* (pp. 376–391). Macmillan.

Rupp, A. (1998). Training of discussion leader and participant behavior or the development of communicative competence in discussions. In H. G. Klinzing (Ed.), *New learning methods: Zweite Festschrift für Walter Zifreund* (pp. 357–375). dgvt-Verlag.

Rupp, A. (2010). Online discussion—Some recommendations for action. In A. Rupp (Ed.), *Moderne Konzepte in der betrieblichen und universitären Aus- und Weiterbildung*. [Modern concepts in vocational and university education and training. Festschrift for Hans Gerhard Klinzing] (3rd ed.) (pp. 145–161). dgtv-Verlag.

Rupp, A. (2013). Interpersonal and communicative competence in online and face-to-face (seminar) discussions—An experimental study. In B. Jürgens & G. Krause (Eds.), *Professionalization through training* (pp. 157–171). Shaker Verlag.

Rupp, A. (2015). *Adaptive teaching*. [Unpublished training material. Center for New Learning Methods, University of Tübingen].

Rupp, A. (2019). Improving leadership communication competencies and skills through training. In V. Hammler Kenon, & S. V. Palsone (Eds.), *The Wiley handbook of global workplace learning* (pp. 447–476). Wiley Blackwell.

Rupp, A. (2021). Utveckla ledarskapet genom mikroundervisning—enligt modellen för struktueread undervisning [Developing leadership skills through microteaching—the structured learning model]. In M. Karlberg & M. Samuelsson (Eds.), *Ledarskap, Social Realtioner och Konflikthantering för Lärrare* (pp. 179–204). Författarna och Natur & Kultur.

Rupp, A., & Klinzing, H. G. (1999). *Direct instruction. Microteaching training course*. [Unpublished training material. Center for New Learning Methods, University of Tübingen].

Rupp, A., & Klinzing, H. G. (2008). *Direct instruction model. Microteaching training course*. [Unpublished training material. Center for New Learning Methods, University of Tübingen].

Schiefele, U., Krapp, A., & Schreyer, I. (1993). Meta-analysis of the relationship between interest and academic achievement. *Journal of Developmental and Educational Psychology*, 25(2), 120–148.

Schön, D. A. (1987). *Educating the reflective practitioner: Toward a new design for teaching and learning in the professions*. Jossey-Bass.

Sharan, S., Sharan, Y., & Tan, I. G.-C. (2013). The group investigation approach to cooperative learning. In C. E. Hmelo-Silver, C. A. Chinn, C. K. K. Chan, & A. O'Donnell (Eds.), *The international handbook of collaborative learning* (pp. 351–369). Routledge.

Sharan, Y., & Sharan, S. (1992). *Expanding cooperative learning through group investigation*. Teachers College Press.

Shimanoff, S. B. (1980). *Communication rules: Theory and research*. SAGE Publications.

Slavin, R. E. (1983). *Cooperative learning*. Longman.

Slavin, R. E. (2006). *Educational psychology theory and practice* (8th ed.). Pearson Education.

Smith, L. R., & Cotten, M. L. (1980). Effect of lesson vagueness and discontinuity on student achievement and attitudes. *Journal of Educational Psychology*, *72*(5), 670–675. https://doi.org/10.1037/0022-0663.72.5.670

Spitzberg, B. H. (1988). Communication competence: Measures of perceived effectiveness. In C. H. Tardy (Ed.), *A handbook for the study of human communication*. Ablex.

Schulz-Hardt, S., & Brodbeck, F. C. (2014). Group performance and leadership. In K. Jonas, W. Stroebe, & M. Hewstone (Eds.), *Social psychology* (pp. 469–505). Springer.

Steiner, I. D. (1972). *Group processes and productivity*. Academic Press.

Szpunar, K. K., Khan, N. Y., & Schacter, D. L. (2013). Interpolated memory tests reduce mind wandering and improve learning of online lectures. *Psychological and Cognitive Sciences*, *110*(16), 6313–6317. https://doi.org/10.1073/pnas.1221764110

Tausch, R., & Tausch, A. (1998). *Educational psychology* (11th ed.). Hogrefe.

Tomasello, M. (2020). *Becoming human. A theory of ontogenesis*. Suhrkamp.

Van Dijk, L. A., van den Berg, G. C., & van Keulen, H. (2001). Interactive lectures in engineering education. *European Journal of Engineering Education*, *26*(1), 15–28. https://doi.org/doi.abs/10.1080/03043790123124

Ventis, W. L., Higbee, G., & Murdock, S. A. (2001). Using humor in systematic desensitization to reduce fear. *The Journal of General Psychology*, *128*(2), 241–253. https://doi.org/10.1080/00221300109598911

Watzlawick, P., Beavin, J., & Jackson, D. (1985). *Human communication. Forms, disturbances, paradoxes*. Hans Huber.

Wiemann, J. M. (1977). Explication and test of a model of communicative competence. *Human Communication Research*, *3*(3), 195–213. https://doi.org/10.1111/j.1468-2958.1977.tb00518.x

Wiemann, J. M., & Bradac, J. J. (1989). Metatheoretical issues in the study of communication competence: Structural and functional approaches. In B. Dervin & M. J. Vight (Eds.), *Progress in communication sciences* (Vol. 9, pp. 261–284). Ablex.

Wiemann, J. M., & Giles, H. (1992). Interpersonal communication. In W. Stroebe, M. Hewstone, J. P. Codol, & G. M. Stephenson (Eds.), *Social psychology* (2nd corrected ed., pp. 209–230). Springer.

Woolfolk, A. (2014). *Educational psychology* (14th ed.). Pearson.

Wubbels, T., Brekelmans, M., den Brok, P., & van Tartwijk, J. (2006). An interpersonal perspective on classroom management in secondary classrooms in the Netherlands. In C. M. Evertson & C. S. Weinstein (Eds.), *Handbook of classroom management: Research, practice, and contemporary issues* (pp. 1161–1191). Lawrence Erlbaum Associates Publishers.

Zifreund, W. (1966). *Concept for training teaching behavior with television recordings in small group seminars*. Cornelsen.

Ziv, A. (2008). Teaching and learning with humor. *The Journal of Experimental Education*, *57*(1), 4–15. https://doi.org/10.1080/00220973.1988.10806492

# Index

Ability: to use and analyze theoretical background knowledge, to use conceptual structures, to form hypotheses, to perform actions, to use feedback  3, 141, 142, 143
Achievement  65, 112, 114, 117, 164, 168
Adaptive teaching  131, 132, 134, 135, 141, 150, 171
Affiliation: respect, humor, openness, friendliness, encouragement  17, 62, 68, 69

Behavioral dimension: clarity, motivation and interest, social learning climate and social atmosphere  8, 15, 16, 17, 19, 47, 61, 147
Buzzgroups  106

Case method  119, 121
Case study  31, 34
Clarity  16, 17, 19, 28, 29, 34, 36, 126, 127, 152
Communication  3, 38, 55, 62, 67, 78, 81, 141
Conditions: external  13
Cooperative learning  99, 124

Culture  3, 4, 33, 95

Demonstration  141, 142
Direct instruction  130, 151
Discussion leader  124, 125, 126, 127, 128, 129, 130
Discussion: skills  125, 126, 128

Encouragement  68, 73, 74, 128, 149, 163
Engagement  16, 49, 51, 53, 54, 66, 118
Enthusiasm  16, 17, 47, 55, 58, 59, 77, 153, 154
Evaluation: assessment, tests, examinations, learning success  107, 112, 113, 137, 116, 147, 164, 169

Facial expression  32, 33, 39, 58, 59, 75, 76, 77, 78, 79, 81, 82
Feedback  53, 54, 101, 106, 130, 132, 136, 140, 141, 142, 143, 143, 149, 156, 164, 166
Flexibility: monitoring, transitions, relationship with individuals and group  147, 160

# INDEX

Friendliness 62, 66, 68, 72, 73, 75, 149, 162, 165

Gaze/eye contact 33, 75, 76, 77, 78, 79, 81, 126
Gestures 13, 31, 32, 39, 58, 59, 75, 76, 81, 82, 83, 126, 154
Group performance 99
Group tournament 115

Humor 55, 57, 58, 62, 67, 68, 70, 71, 133, 154

Interactive: presentation 30, 118, 122, 130, 133, 137, 147, 150

Jigsaw 104, 112, 113, 114, 115

Knowledge: apply, acquiring, background, communication of, deepening, existing, gaps in, imparting, organization of, transfer, integration of, professional 3, 4, 5, 6, 7, 10, 12, 15, 16, 22, 29, 33, 34, 37, 49, 86, 94, 99, 108, 109, 120, 123, 125, 134, 135, 139, 141, 146, 152, 153, 166, 171

Liveliness: verbal, non-verbal 50, 55, 58, 59, 77

Macro level 134
Micro level 134, 136
Microteaching: concept, training program 131, 132, 137, 139, 140, 142, 143, 145, 146, 151, 171
Monitoring 54, 101, 102, 104, 107, 111, 113, 116, 143, 149, 158, 160
Motivation: individual interest, situational interest 7, 8, 9, 15, 16, 29, 47, 48, 49, 50, 52, 53, 58, 61, 85, 112, 100, 153, 163

Non-verbal behavior 59, 75, 77, 79, 80, 81, 82, 83

Objectives: learning, specifics, general 9, 10, 11, 14, 16, 130, 139, 141
Openness 62, 68, 71, 77, 79, 135

Planning 8, 9, 16, 51, 52, 111, 139, 141, 150

Posture 32, 33, 39, 53, 59, 68, 70, 72, 75, 76, 78, 79, 154
Practicing: questions 40, 42, 158
Praise 63, 64, 66, 73, 74, 99, 128, 166, 168

Questions 11, 29, 36, 39, 40, 42, 52, 54, 63, 64, 65, 71, 72, 78, 101, 106, 108, 112, 117, 118, 119, 125, 126, 127, 134, 153, 154, 155, 159, 166, 167

Recognition 52, 63, 69, 103, 112, 114, 117, 128, 164, 166, 168
Respect 17, 62, 65, 66, 67, 68, 69, 130
Rules: communication rules, flexible, explicit 15, 34, 52, 62, 64, 66, 67, 68, 76, 78, 101, 105, 107, 109, 113, 115, 125, 129, 158

Skills: effectiveness, appropriateness, for clarity, for classroom management, for interest, for rules, for social learning climate 8, 17, 29, 31, 36, 40, 48, 50, 51, 52, 63, 66, 68, 69, 70, 71, 72, 72, 73, 143, 145
Social learning climate: control, dominance, social-integrative, submission 61, 62, 63, 66, 124
Spatial behavior 75, 76, 79, 81, 118
Structure: hierarchical, linear sequential, network 16, 17, 20, 21, 22, 24, 27, 29, 88
Subject content 16, 99, 132, 133, 134, 150, 158

Target audience 11, 88
Teaching: adaptive, methods, subject content, interactive 4, 5, 6, 8, 14, 99, 130, 134
Training program: planning, selection of methods 131, 132, 137, 139, 140, 149, 169, 149, 151, 171

Variation: combination of methods 136, 147, 150, 151, 153
Visualizations: functions of, diagrams, dealing with data, slide design 28, 40, 85, 153

Work structure 102, 105

Adelswärd, I. 57
Allen, D. W. 140
Allodi, M. W. 61
Anderson, J. R. 23, 108
Argyle, M. 16, 62, 63, 66, 67, 75, 76, 147
Ausubel, D. P. 22

Barkley, E. F. 16, 17
Barnett, J. 54
Bateson, G. 61
Berliner, D. C. 16
Biggs, J. 133
Black, P. 164
Bligh, D. A. 6, 7, 16, 19
Bloom, B. S. 10, 16
Borich, G. 42, 61, 62, 63, 64, 67, 70, 74, 156
Bradac, J. J. 71
Brekelmans, M. 17, 62, 68
Bretschneider, V. 121
Bridges, D. 129
Brodbeck, F. C. 100
Brophy, J. E. 66, 168
Burgoon, J. 62
Buskist, W. 17

Cain, J. 54
Celik, T. 53
Chen, C.-H. 70
Chilcoat, G. W. 29, 31, 32, 33, 36, 37, 38, 42
Corno, L. 134, 136, 147
Cotten, M. L. 38
Cruickshank, D. R. 58, 134, 141

Daniel, B. K. 53
DeVito, J. A. 71
Dohn, N. B. 50
Duarte, N. 87, 90, 94

Easton, G. 55
Ekman, P. 76, 77
Ellis, D. 53
Emmer, E. T. 129
Evertson, C. M. 129

Floden, R. E. 140
Fogelgarn, R. 52
Freeman, S. 7
Furnham, A. 67

Gage, N. 16
Gall, M. D. 122, 123
Giles, H. 68
Goffman, E. 69
Gregory, J. L. 54
Grimm Brothers 24

Hale, J. 61
Hall, E. T. 79
Hall, R. H. 54
Halperin, E. 70
Hattie, J. 9, 166, 168
Hewes, G. 81
Hidi, S. 47
Hiller, J. A. 38
Hofstadter, D. 35

Jameson Boex, L. F. 16
Jang, H. 49
Johnson, D. W. 102
Johnson, R. T. 102
Joyce, B. 5

Kaess, W. 38
Kaiser, F. J. 121
Kay, R. H. 54
Keller, M. M. 58
Kelley, J. W. 17
Klein, R. 53
Klinzing, H. G. 5, 16, 17, 19, 61, 140, 141, 169
Kounin, J. S. 160
Kroeber-Riel, W. 87

LeSage, A. 54
Lewis, R. 51, 52

Mager, R. 10
Mayor, C. H. 16, 17

McKeachie, W. J. 7
Mehrabian, A. 79
Merseth, K. K. 120
Metcalf, K. K. 57, 141
Mueller, P. A. 40

Nir, N. 70
Nkomo, L. M. 53

Öberg, B. M. 57
Oliveira, C. G. 52
Oliveira, P. C. 52
Oppenheimer, D. M. 40

Provalis Research 39

Randi, J. 134
Reed, D. K. 40
Renninger, K. A. 47
Reyes-Fournier, E. 17
Rogers, C. R. 68
Rosenshine, B. 130, 151

Rupp, A. 16, 17, 62, 68, 122, 123, 124, 130, 131, 147, 151, 169, 170
Ryan, K. A. 140

Sander, E. 35
Schiefele, U. 49

Schön, D. A. 108
Schulz-Hardt, S. 100
Sharan, S. 109
Sharan, Y. 109
Shimanoff, S. B. 67
Slavin, R. E. 112, 114
Smith, L. R. 38
Smith, M. K. 7
Spitzberg, B. H. 164
Steiner, I. D. 136
Stevens, R. 130, 151
Szpunar, K. K. 48

Tausch, A. 62, 63, 68, 69, 74, 162
Tausch, R. 62, 63, 68, 69, 74, 162
Tisher, R. P. 141
Tomasello, M. 3, 4, 81, 82

Van Dijk, L. A. 133
Ventis, W. L. 70

Watzlawick, P. 61, 162
Wiemann, J. M. 68, 71
William. D. 164
Woolfolk, A. 16, 108
Wubbels, T. 51

Zifreund, W. 140
Ziv, A. 70

www.ingramcontent.com/pod-product-compliance
Lightning Source LLC
Chambersburg PA
CBHW061714300426
44115CB00014B/2690